Black's Picture Sports

HANG GLIDING

Black's Picture Sports

HANG GLIDING

DUNSTAN HADLEY

Adam and Charles Black · London

First published 1979 by A & C Black (Publishers) Ltd
35 Bedford Row, London WC1R 4JH

ISBN 0 7136 1914 7

Hadley, Dunstan
Hang gliding.–(Black's picture sports).
1. Hang gliding
I. Title
797.5′5 GV764

ISBN 0-7136-1914-7

Acknowledgements
Cover photo by Waspair
1 East Anglian Daily Times; 2, 3, 4, 5, 8, 9, 10 Erik Hadley; 6 J B McMenemy; 7, 11 Dunstan Hadley; Back cover Patricia Hadley
Line drawings Colin Paine and Erik Hadley

Set and printed in Great Britain by
Page Bros (Norwich) Ltd, Norwich

Contents

Foreword

Hang gliding is fun: it is also dangerous and requires skill and care. Before buying a hang glider, learn to fly one. To qualify for the Hang Glider Pilot's Elementary Certificate, you must carry out 15 satisfactory flights, watched by an official observer appointed by the British Hang Gliding Association.

To obtain further information about the sport, together with a list of BHGA registered flying schools in your area, send a medium-sized, stamped, addressed envelope plus a 50p postal order to: British Hang Gliding Association, 167A Cheddon Road, Taunton, Somerset TA2 7AH.

To fly a hang glider you must be at least fairly fit. A person who is eligible for a driving licence, and who is also able to lift a glider, weighing 40 or 50 lbs, and control it on the ground prior to flight, will probably be fit to fly. People who suffer from a chronic illness or disability may also be able to fly, but they should consult a doctor first.

The minimum age at which a person may fly solo is 16 years.

The theory of flight is not very difficult to understand, and, with care, most people can develop the skills needed for safe and enjoyable hang gliding. As you gain experience, you will come to appreciate that flying is an art – and one which requires considerable delicacy and precision of touch.

1 Equipment

THE GLIDER

A hang glider is an aircraft in which the undercarriage and take off power are provided solely by the legs of the pilot. The glider in flight is pulled towards the ground by the force of gravity. Because of the lift generated by its movement through the air it does not fall straight down, but glides down an invisible slope. Most hang gliders are controlled in flight by the pilot shifting his weight fore and aft or from side to side, although some machines have movable control surfaces, usually hand operated. Some hang gliders may have rigid wings like those of conventional aircraft, others have flexible wings.

The 'Flexwing', designed originally by National Aeronautics and Space Administration (NASA) scientist Dr Francis Rogallo as a steerable parachute for the recovery of rocket nose cones, is the more popular type of the two. It consists of a wing made of sailcloth, supported by a framework of metal tubes, held in position by rigging wires. The pilot is suspended below in a harness and controls the aircraft by exerting pressure on the 'control bar'. This forms an integral part of the aircraft and is a triangular frame to which the lower rigging wires are attached. In flight the wing assumes a shape like two half cones joined to each other along one edge. Variations in design make this basic shape less apparent in the more advanced gliders, where the wing is shaped more like the wing of a conventional aircraft.

Rigid wing hang glider

Advanced Rogallo, pilot using prone harness

PROTECTIVE CLOTHING

When you fly a hang glider, you will be more exposed to the weather and injury than any other kind of aviator. You must therefore wear suitable clothing.

Crash Helmet It is mandatory in Great Britain for the pilot of a hang glider to wear a crash helmet, approved by the BHGA, for competition flying. It is also required by all schools and clubs registered with the BHGA. Any helmet made to British Standards BS 5361 or BS 2495.1977 or their equivalent meets BHGA requirements. Most helmets are made in three or four sizes, though there are some firms which make helmets in more sizes.

Helmets made for rock climbing, canoeing, American ball games, caving, construction work or even service flying are unsuitable for hang gliding.

The helmet protects the brain by absorbing the impact of a crash. It is most important that your helmet fits you properly; it should not allow your head to move freely inside it. A helmet which is too big will, on impact, slip round your head or even come off. The chin strap should fasten under the jaw; don't use a chin cup, it may dislocate your jaw if the helmet is forcibly rotated. Most pilots prefer an open face helmet, and this type is probably best for a beginner. A full face helmet is perhaps more suitable for high altitude flying, as it gives your face better protection from the cold wind. The outside of the helmet must be smooth so that it will slide along a surface, and not rotate. There are some helmets made especially for hang gliding. These either have holes over the ears or leave the ears exposed. Many pilots find that the improvement in hearing is helpful, though not all consider it necessary.

Look after your helmet; don't drop it on a hard surface. If, for any reason, your helmet is damaged, it should be replaced, or returned to the maker for examination before further use. Many pilots like to paint their helmets–if you wish to do this, make sure that the paint will not weaken the helmet, by reacting chemically with the outer shell.

Clothing Flying with a cold, 20 mph wind blowing over your body causes wind-chill, which numbs the senses and stiffens the muscles, as does cold due to low air temperature. Warmth is best maintained by layers of clothing, which will trap air inside and insulate your body. In warm weather many pilots wear light clothing only, but this gives very little protection from abrasion, and if you stay up long or fly high you may get cold, in spite of the sunshine.

It is advisable to wear showerproof garments which are resistant to abrasions (which give protection when landing accidentally on rough surfaces or bushes); a onepiece jumpsuit as worn by parachutists is suitable, as also are the sort of clothes used for motor cycling or skiing.

Gloves It is advisable always to wear strong leather gloves; rose pruning gloves are excellent. They should not be too close fitting, or they will be hot in summer. In winter, a pair of woollen gloves can be worn inside.

Footwear In order to take off, you must run–carrying a rather unmanageable load–over ground which may be rough or slippery. You may land heavily in a ploughed field, and your climb back up the hill may be steep, over ground dotted with mole-hills and rabbit holes. For these reasons, many people wear boots, and there are special ones made for hang gliding which are warm and comfortable. Some other kinds of boots are suitable, but you should not use those which have hooks for the laces, since these may become caught in the rigging wires, or those which come too high up the leg or are stiff–such as ski boots.

The ankle will withstand a lot of strain but if the force is transmitted higher up the leg the bone is more likely to break. When a hang glider is properly flown there is no undue strain on the legs, in either take off or landing, and many pilots wear only light shoes. Once you have learned to fly you will know what sort of footwear is best for you. When you are experienced and start flying higher, you will need fur lined boots if your feet are not to become very cold or frost bitten.

Always dress according to climate, terrain and flight plan, and bear in mind the following advice:

1 Don't leave any flapping laces which might become entangled with the glider.
2 Don't wear a tie or other restrictive clothing.
3 Don't wear a scarf unless it is very well tucked in, or it may flap in your face or catch in the glider.
4 Don't carry sharp or hard objects, such as bottles, in your pockets.

2 Flight

Take off is made straight into wind from a suitable hill. In order to take off, the pilot lifts the glider, to which his harness is attached, and holds it with the nose tilted slightly upwards. He then runs directly into wind. As he runs he rotates the nose of the glider further upwards by pushing on the control bar. The wing now meets the airstream at an angle called the 'angle of attack'. The sail fills and the aerofoil shape is formed.

As the wing is moving forwards the airstream divides at the leading edge, some air passing over the wing and some underneath. Because of the curved shape of the wing, the air going over the top has further to travel to reach the trailing edge than the air passing beneath, which tends to pass in a straight line from leading to trailing edge rather than follow the curve under the wing. The air flowing over the top must therefore go faster, so that it arrives at the trailing edge at the same time as the air passing below. If it did not, the air from below would curl up over the trailing edge of the wing. The increase in speed of the airstream over the top results in a fall in pressure over the upper surface of the wing, known as the 'Bernoulli effect'. The air pressure beneath the wing pushes the aircraft upwards into the low pressure area formed, thus creating 'lift', and the pilot is lifted off the ground. Much more than half the lift created by the wing is produced by the reduced pressure above, which 'sucks it up'. The rest is due to the increase of pressure below it, caused by the forward motion of the wing through the air, and to atmospheric pressure.

The lift is dependent on a smooth flow of air over the upper surface of the wing. The amount of lift created depends on the angle of attack, the shape of the wing and the speed of the aircraft.

As the angle of attack is increased, the aircraft speed will decrease, because of the increase in 'drag' caused by the wing passing through the air at a greater angle.

Lift will also increase until at a certain angle, the 'stalling angle', the airstream is no longer able to maintain its smooth flow over the wing and begins to break

Figure 1 Deflection of airstream over wing

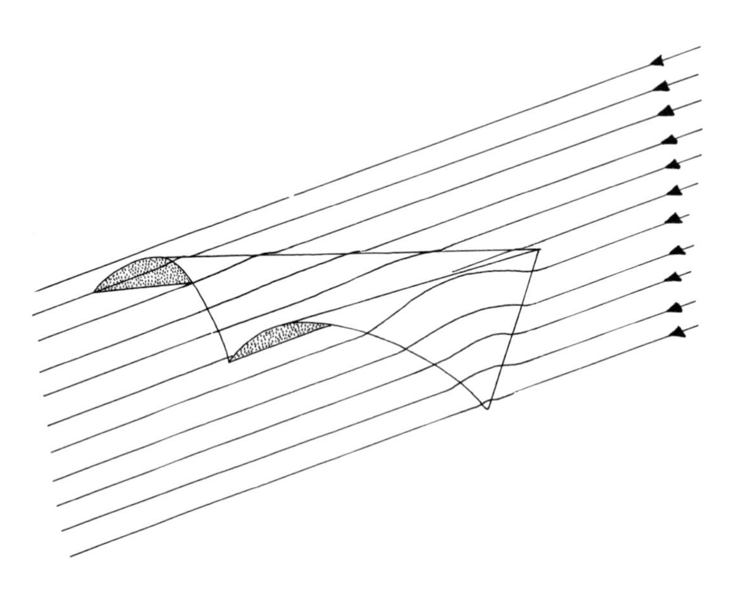

Figure 2 Normal airstream

up. As the air creeps up over the trailing edge causing eddies and turbulence, air rushes in from behind, the low pressure area is destroyed and the wing stalls. With no lift to keep it up, the aircraft drops. To regain control, the pilot must pull on the control bar to decrease the angle of attack, and increase speed, so that the smooth airstream will reform, and the lift will be restored.

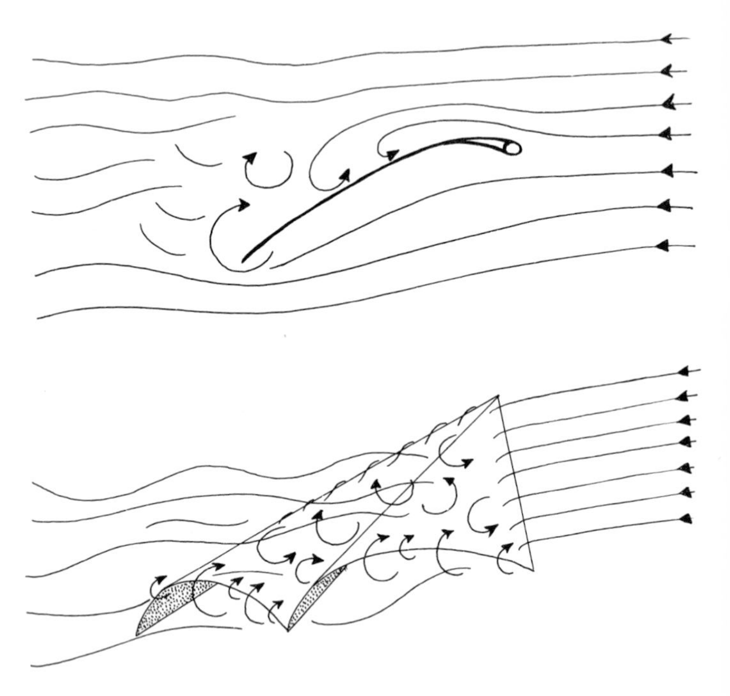

Figure 3 Airstream in stall

The airspeed at which the stall occurs depends on the total weight of the aircraft. A heavy pilot stalls at the same angle of attack as would a lighter pilot flying the same glider, but at a higher speed. If the aircraft is in a turn, or pulling out of a dive, it is following a curved path. The centrifugal force created by the curved line of flight increases the load to be supported by increasing the apparent weight of the aircraft. To demonstrate this, swing a weight on a string round your head: as you swing the weight faster you will feel the increase in the pull on the string. The wing still stalls at the same angle of attack but because of the apparent increase in weight the airspeed will be higher. Therefore the pilot must pull in the control bar to increase speed before making a turn to allow for the higher 'stalling speed'. The average speed at which a hang glider in level flight will stall is about 8–15 mph. In a turn, the stalling speed will be perhaps 20 mph in a gentle turn, and even up to 25–35 mph in a steep, tight turn.

When the aircraft stalls, a lot of height may be lost before the pilot can regain control. Stalling must therefore only be attempted when there is sufficient height to recover (see also page 45). One exception to this rule is landing. In order to land, the aircraft is flown close to and parallel with the ground. As the speed falls, the control bar is gently eased forward, raising the nose of the aircraft until it stalls with the pilot only a foot or two above the ground.

It is vitally important to understand the difference between airspeed and groundspeed.

Airspeed is the speed of the aircraft *through the air*. The aircraft may be travelling in any direction over the ground and at any groundspeed, or upwards or downwards. Airspeed must always be maintained in order to control the aircraft in flight.

Groundspeed is the speed of the aircraft over the ground. For example, an aircraft flying at an airspeed of 20 mph directly into a wind of 15 mph will be travelling over the ground at 5 mph. If it now turns to fly downwind, at the same airspeed, it will be flying with a speed over the ground (or groundspeed) of 35 mph. The pilot turning to fly downwind must not be deceived into thinking that he is going too fast, and slow down, or the aircraft will stall. He must always keep airspeed above stalling speed in order to retain control. As the pilot obviously wants to touch down at as slow a groundspeed as possible, he always makes his landing into wind. Flying across the wind direction, the aircraft will move diagonally across the ground. This movement is known as 'drift' and does not affect the airspeed. (See section on landing, page 34.)

CONTROL IN FLIGHT

After taking off the aircraft glides downward, in still air, along a path at an angle to the horizontal known as the 'glide angle'. This angle depends on the shape of the wing and the position in which it is held by the pilot to control the speed. The weight of the aircraft which is pulling it down, according to Newton's law, is balanced by an equal and opposite reaction holding it up. The forces of lift and weight pull the aircraft along its glide path, while the resistance of the air, known as 'drag', holds it back from going as fast as it otherwise would. These forces balance to give the aircraft a constant speed. By using trigonometry, the lift/drag or L/D ratio can be worked out (Figure 4). Expressed simply, if the glider glides 8 ft forwards each time it sinks 1 ft downwards, the L/D ratio is 8/1. 8/1 is a reasonable L/D ratio for a hang glider.

In a straight glide, a correctly trimmed aircraft will glide without the pilot exerting any pressure on the control bar. This is because the lift acts on the glider through one point known as the centre of lift or C of L. This is positioned exactly over the centre of gravity or C of G of the whole aircraft and pilot (Figure 5). If the pilot now pulls on the bar he pulls his weight, and therefore the C of G, forward of the C of L and this tilts the nose of the glider down. The glide therefore becomes steeper, the airspeed increases, until, as the drag also increases, equilibrium is reached and a steady but higher speed is maintained. Pushing on the bar has the opposite effect.

The best glide is obtained when the aircraft travels the furthest distance for the height lost. This optimum performance occurs at a certain airspeed in any given

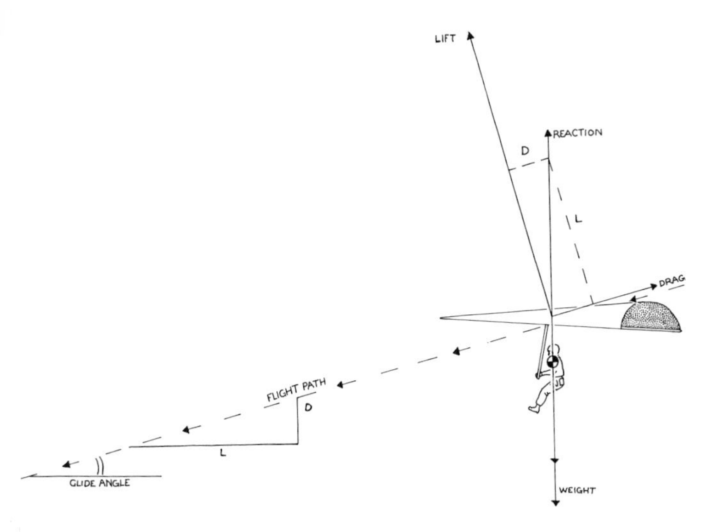

Figure 4 Lift/drag ratio. The total reaction to the weight is divided into lift and drag. The same proportions represent the distance gained for height lost in still air. The lift and the weight between them produce the forward motion. The resistance of the air causes the drag

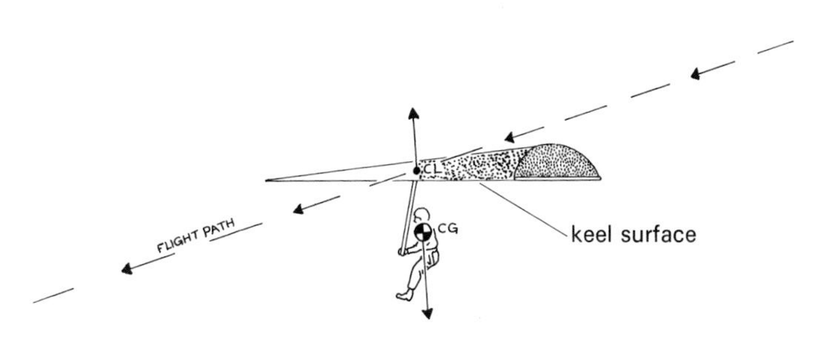

Figure 5 Centre of lift and centre of gravity. Lift occurs all over the wing, but mostly over the area one third of the way back from the leading edge. The point through which all the lift acting together is assumed to operate is known as the centre of lift. This point moves slightly fore and aft as the angle of attack varies. The weight of the pilot and glider together is centred at a point below the keel boom known as the centre of gravity. Keel surface is all the surface of the aircraft and pilot exposed to sideways motion. As the aircraft slips sideways, the keel surface behind the centre of gravity (being larger than the area in front) causes the tail to be held back, allowing the nose to turn in the direction of slip.

aircraft. It is arrived at not by calculation but by experment, either in flight or in wind tunnel. In order to make a turn, the pilot moves his body to one side. This causes the C of G to move to that side of the C of L. The wing on that side tilts down as the opposite wing rises. The aircraft is 'banked', and this banking causes the aircraft to slip sideways. Because the keel surface of the aircraft is larger behind the C of G than in front, the airstream now hitting this surface causes the nose to turn in the direction of bank and slip. At the same time the pilot exerts gentle pressure on the control bar, pushing the nose up which, because the aircraft is now banked, also means partly turning.

In order to stop the turn, the pilot shifts his weight back to the centre, thus levelling the wings and slightly lowering the nose. For a sustained turn, some modification of this technique is required, as will be described later (see page 50). It is important to understand that in a turn, the inside wing is travelling more slowly than the outside wing and therefore creates less lift. The outside wing, going faster, gives more lift. This means that the inside wing will stall, if the aircraft is allowed to fly too slowly, or the bank reduced too much, while the outside wing is still flying. This may cause a spin. If this happens, pull in the bar to increase speed and regain control. Steep turns near the ground are dangerous because if a stall or spin occurs, there is insufficient height to recover.

3 Take Off

PRE-FLIGHT CHECK

You have now learnt a little of the theory of flight. You are properly clothed and wearing your crash helmet. Your instructor has shown you how to rig the glider. You must now carry out a 'pre-flight check'. Do this before every flight. Even if the previous flight only lasted five seconds, entailing take off and crash landing six feet down the hill, the glider may well have been damaged. Make your inspection in a systematic way.

Start at the Nose

1 Check nose plates to see that they are not bent or cracked, and that fastenings are secure.
2 Check that rigging wires are not frayed, kinked or corroded. Ferrules should be secure and not slipping. Tangs should not be cracked or cutting wires. Wires should not be twisted and should be attached to correct anchorages, and correctly adjusted for tension, top and bottom. Wires must not snag on projections.
3 Check keel boom curves and keel and leading edge booms for abnormal bends or cracks, especially near bolt holes.
4 Examine sail anchorages.

Port Wing

1 Check the fastenings.
2 Check the wires and rigging, as at the nose.

3 Check that the deflexors, if fitted, are properly adjusted.
4 Check cross boom for bends, kinks or cracks.
5 Check that the sail is not pinched in the fastenings.
6 Check that the tip anchorage is secure.

Tail

1 Check the wires and rigging, as at the nose.
2 Check that the settings correspond to those set at the nose.
3 Check sail anchorage.

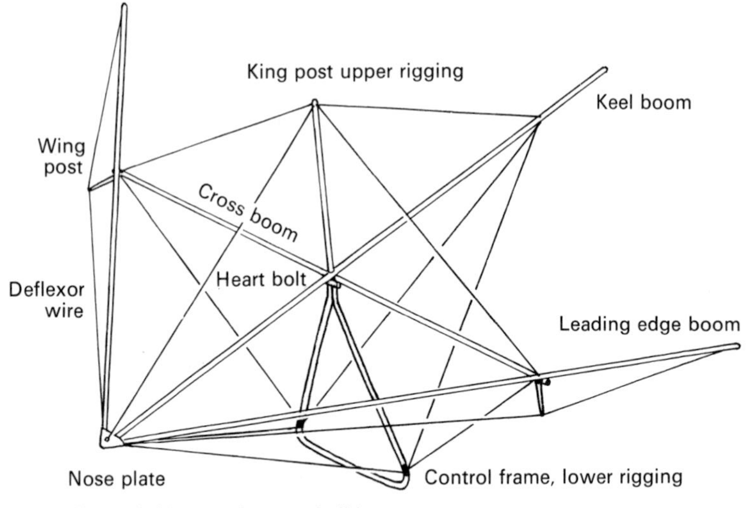

Figure 6 Names of parts of glider

Starboard Wing

Check as for the port side. Check that adjustment is the same as on the port wing, or the wing will probably be twisted and dangerous to fly.

Control Bar

1 Check the heart bolt and associated components.
2 Check the control bar for bends.
3 Check the rigging wire anchorages.
4 Check the harness attachment point.

5 Check whether the rigging is adjusted for seated or prone flight.

Sail

1 Check the stitching and fastenings.
2 Check to see whether there are any tears or holes.

King Post

Check that this is erect, and that the wires are correctly adjusted.

Harness

Check stitching, wear and attachment points.

Fittings

Check fittings exclusive to your glider (altimeter etc).

This may seem a long list. With practice it can easily be done in two minutes, and your life depends on it.

You, and the glider, are now ready to fly.

PREPARATION

For your first flight choose a slope a little steeper than the glide angle of your aircraft. The manufacturer or your instructor will tell you what this is. Start flying near the bottom. You need a wind of about 5–10 mph, not more, blowing without gusts straight towards the hill. You may have to wait some time for exactly the right conditions.

Hang gliding requires great patience and self control. Never be persuaded into doing anything against your better judgement: it might be fatal.

The next steps to take are as follows:

1 Fasten your helmet.
2 Attach the harness securely to yourself and to the glider. Use a seated harness–prone flying comes later. A friend, known as a 'wireman' holds the nose wires to prevent the glider being blown over backwards in a 'ground loop'. He will also help you to

Crouching in position

support the nose at the correct angle for take off. Put a foot on the bottom bar and pull the sides of the control bar towards you. This will bring the nose up to the take off position.

3 Check that no one is climbing the hill just below you.

4 Check the windspeed and direction. Ask your wireman to throw a small handful of grass into the air. If it is blown straight back towards you the wind direction is correct. The speed can be estimated or measured with a ventimeter (see Chapter 7).

Lift the glider and stand upright. Hold the glider in the way that you find best for control. A popular method is to hold the bottom bar with one hand, holding the upright on one side with the other.

5 Check that there are no obstructions, fences, high tension or telephone wires in your intended flight path.

6 Check that there are no spectators, children, or dogs in the way.

7 Check that there are no gliders just about to fly across your take off path.

If your wireman says 'Are you ready?' and you are not, say 'Stop'. The use of standard words and phrases prevents confusion. 'Go' and 'no' sound too much alike. Do not take off unless you are quite ready – take off requires determination and complete confidence that you will be successful. Think it through beforehand, until you have the action perfectly clear in your mind. You can rest the glider on your shoulders or thighs and be quite comfortable for 10 minutes or so, waiting for the wind to be just right. Having got this far it takes more courage not to fly than to fly. If you are not satisfied with the conditions fold your wings and go home.

TAKE OFF

The sequence is as follows (Figure 7):

1 Face directly into wind.

2 Lift the aircraft until the harness straps are taut.

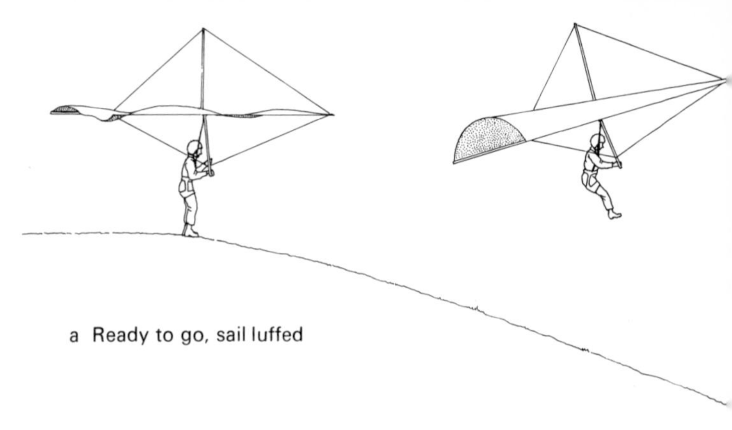

a Ready to go, sail luffed

b Run full speed, push on bar to be lifted off

Figure 7 Taking off

3 Tilt the nose slightly above the horizontal, about 5° for most gliders. This you do by telling your wireman, who is facing you and holding the nose wires, to come closer, until you judge the angle to be correct.
4 When you are quite ready call 'Release'. The wireman releases the wires and ducks out of the way.
5 Then go-go-go! Run forward, accelerating smoothly, so as not to upset the angle of the wing. After five or six steps you are going at full speed.
6 Push forward on the control bar and you will be lifted up. Do this with enthusiasm. Do not jump: just keep running until your feet leave the ground.

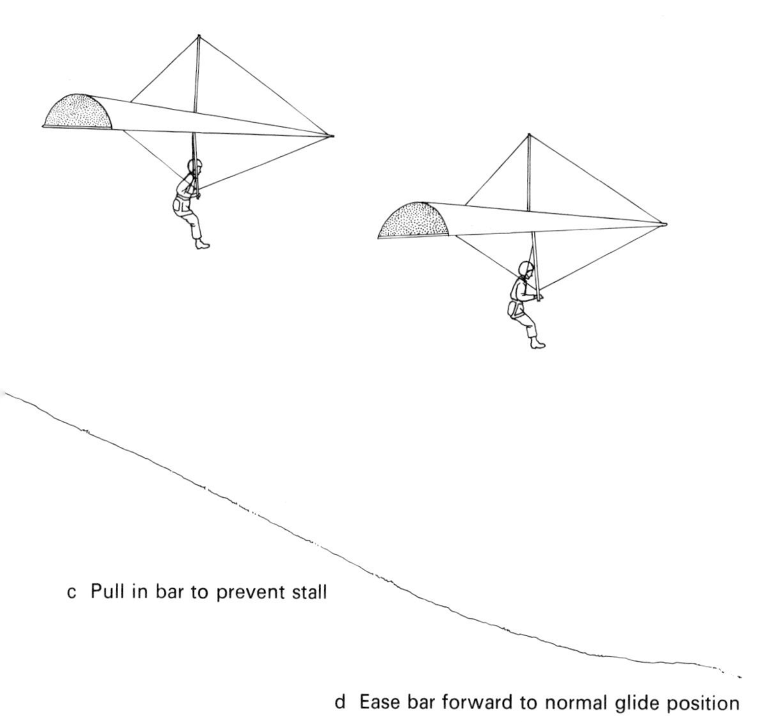

c Pull in bar to prevent stall

d Ease bar forward to normal glide position

7 As soon as you are flying, at once ease the bar towards you slightly to prevent a stall (caused by rotating the nose up for take off). At the same time move your upper hand down to the bottom bar.
8 Straighten in a steady glide.

Always remember that you are not running off a hill into space, but running to gain speed. As soon as the glider has sufficient speed, tip up the nose to make it fly and it will take you up with it. The ground only begins to fall away when you are being lifted up, securely held in your harness. Do not be casual or half-hearted about your take off: try to make it perfect every time. If you become careless, you will pay for it.

Holding the wires (note position of pilot's hands)

Almost ready to go, straps not yet taut

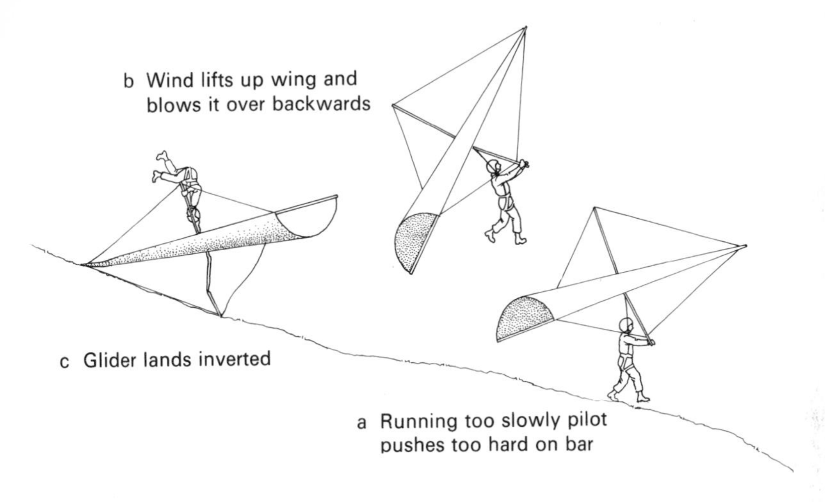

Figure 8 Ground loop

LIKELY MISTAKES

1 Run too slowly, and the aircraft will topple forward, the wind will strike the top of the sail and push the nose into the ground, or you will fall over; or both.
2 Don't push the nose up too soon – the drag caused by the inflated wing will be so great that you will be unable to gain enough speed before your feet leave the ground. You will either take off, stall and immediately fall back to the ground or, if the wind is strong, the glider will be blown over backwards in a ground loop (Figure 8). This may hurt you and will probably damage the aircraft by bending one of the booms, or the king post, as it lands upside down. It may also injure a spectator.
3 Take off with one wing low and the aircraft will start to turn as soon as you are airborne. At the low speed at which you are flying, the inside wing is likely to stall and turn you back into the hill at high speed.

c Slow speed and poor lift on inside wing leads to turn tightening or wing stalling. Aircraft dives into hill

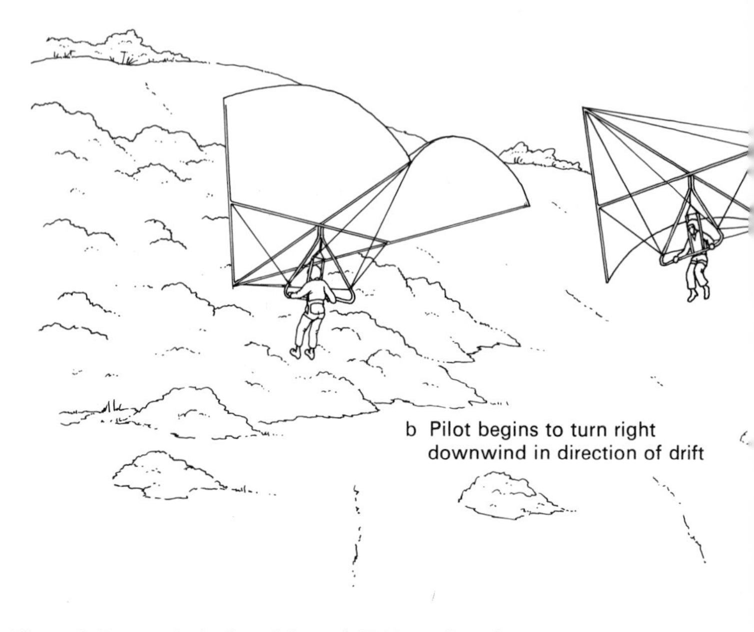

Figure 9 Cross-wind take off hazard. Taking off with one wing low may have the same result

DIFFICULT WIND CONDITIONS

Cross-wind When you take off in a cross-wind, because the wind is blowing slightly across the face of the hill, there will be much less lift and you will tend to sink much more rapidly after take off.

As soon as you take off, you will start to drift sideways. If the drift is not corrected immediately you may hit an obstruction, which you would have missed on a normal take off into wind. If you make an inadvertent landing while drifting, you are much more likely to hurt your knees or ankles or damage the aircraft.

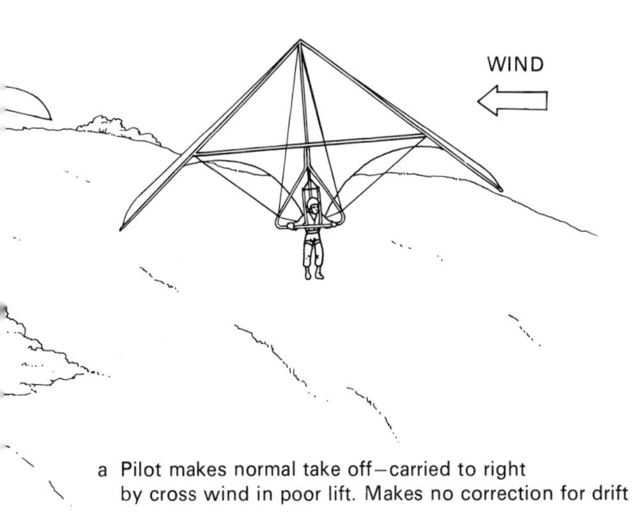

a Pilot makes normal take off—carried to right by cross wind in poor lift. Makes no correction for drift

Gusts Beware of gusts. Test the wind with a special meter, a ventimeter, before you take off. If the wind is gusting more than 5 mph for 10 seconds at a time, do not take off. If the wind is gusting 5 mph to 15 mph, it is more dangerous than a 20 mph wind gusting to 25 mph. Stay on the ground–you can always fly another day.

Strong Wind As you become more experienced, you will take off in stronger winds. When the wind speed is 18 mph you will scarcely need to run at all. You must be careful to keep the glider level, with the sail luffed until you are ready to go. Always have a wireman at the nose to prevent an accidental ground loop. It is advisable to run at least one or two steps before you push forward the bar to take off. It will help you to 'penetrate' the wind.

d Throws legs forward to increase speed
and starts to dive. Speed increase is still insufficient

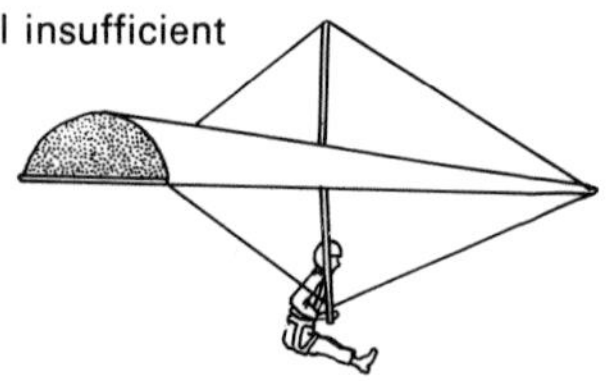

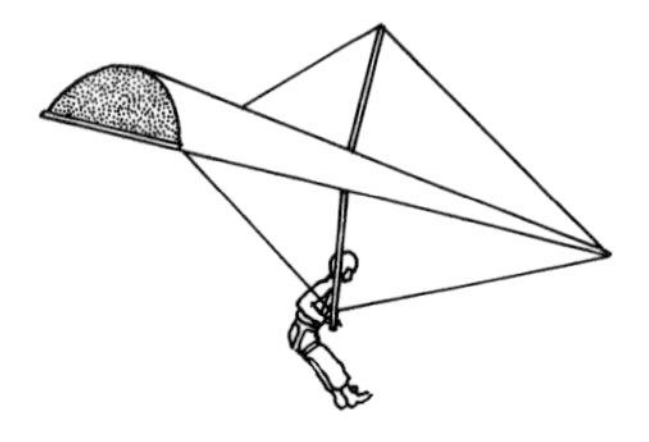

e Glider, now in area of turbulence
and no updraft begins to come down fast

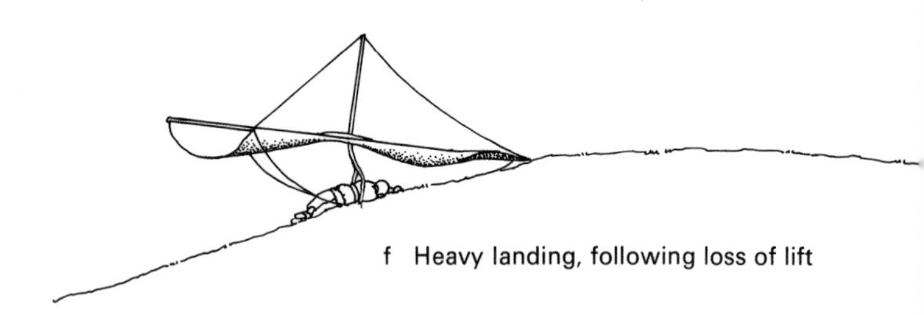

f Heavy landing, following loss of lift

Figure 10 Being blown back

c Pulls in bar to check stall. Airspeed normal but less than windspeed, glider moving backwards over ground

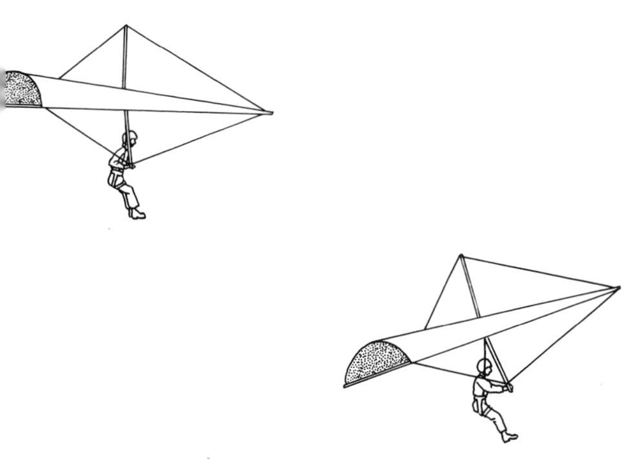

b Pilot takes off and climbs rapidly

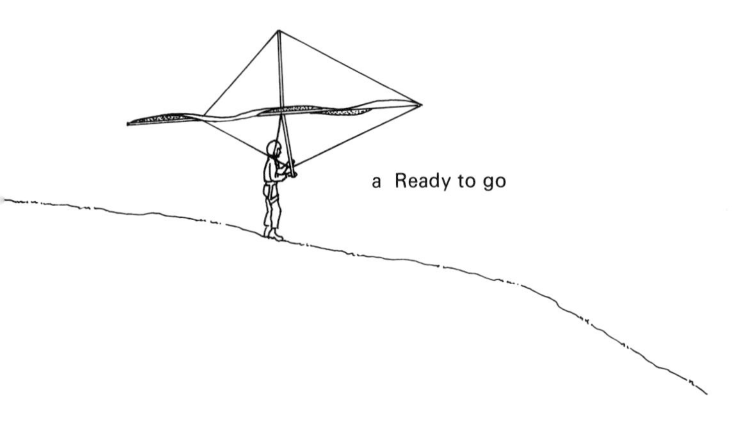

a Ready to go

Do not push out quite so hard as usual, and be ready to pull in a little quicker; and, if necessary, to throw your weight forwards at once to prevent yourself being blown back, or stalling. Do not attempt to take off in a wind over 18 mph until you have much more experience, as the technique is different.

4 Landing

In your early flights, landing comes so soon after take off that as soon as you are airborne you must immediately prepare to land. To begin with you will make bad landings, simply because there is no time to make a proper approach – the basis of a good one. As your flights become a little longer you will begin to enjoy the thrills of real flying, and you might tend to forget that you need to land at all – and swoop in unprepared, landing too fast, and falling over.

WIND GRADIENT

The air flowing close to the ground is slowed by friction. This effect is known as the 'wind gradient' and often extends up to a height of 50 ft, sometimes more. As you descend you will pass through layers of more slowly moving air. Because you are descending fairly quickly, your airspeed may fall off rapidly as you meet the slower airstream and, if you are flying too close to stalling speed, you will stall too high, perhaps with insufficient height to recover. For this reason, your approach speed is kept a little above stalling speed. If the stalling speed of your aircraft is 15 mph, make your approach at an airspeed of 20 mph. This will give you a little speed in reserve when you need it.

How do you know you are flying at 20 mph? Without

instruments, only judgement and experience can tell you. There are two things to guide you:

1 Your instructor or the manufacturer's notes will have told you the stalling speed of your aircraft.
2 Try to remember how fast you seemed to be going when you came in for your first few landings, or how it feels to travel in a car at 20 mph.

If you fly just a little faster than the speed at which you made your first few haphazard landings, you will be about right, remembering that your speed will seem less when you are higher above the ground, and also if the wind is a little stronger.

LANDING SEQUENCE

When you land, you should fly directly into the wind, which will normally be in the same direction as it was for your take off. If your approach line is not quite right, allow yourself sufficient time to make your turn into wind. If you leave it too late, you will pull out of the turn too low to straighten up properly before you touch down.

The proper way to land is to start the approach in good time – the whole sequence can be divided into four phases: the approach, the flare out, the landing, and the touch down, lasting about half a minute altogether.

The Approach The ideal approach is a steady, straight glide, when you are still between 50 and 100 ft up, with 20 or 30 seconds flying time left. This gives you time to assess the situation and get ready for the next stage. Remember to check that you are flying into the wind.

The Flare Out When you reach a height of about 30 ft, you start the flare out by putting a gentle pressure on the control bar, to ease it away from you. This will start to flatten your glide, while still allowing you to descend. (How do you know when you are at 30 ft? Practice will help, but a useful tip is as follows: as you make your approach, the grass looks like a green blur. As soon as you can see the individual blades of grass you are at

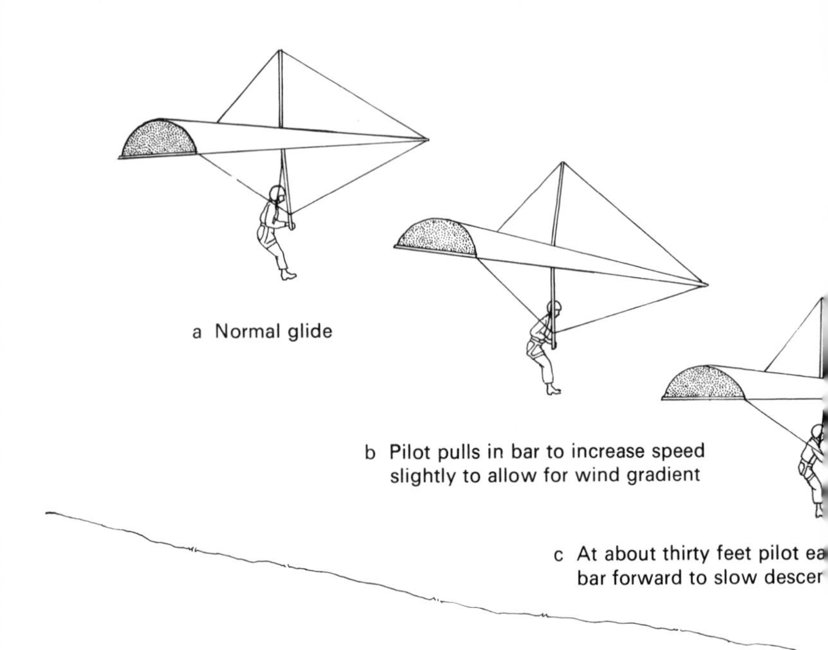

Figure 11 Landing sequence

30 ft. Over surfaces other than grass, watch for the point when the surface comes into sharp focus.) Maintain the pressure on the bar, and as you come down, increase it gradually to slow your descent until you are flying parallel to the ground with your feet about 2 ft above it. Hold it there.

The Landing The aircraft will gradually slow down and eventually stall on to the ground. As this happens, continue to push the bar away from you–not too fast or you will gain height–but with ever increasing thrust. Try to *hold the aircraft off* the ground for as long as possible,

d Bar eased further forward until glider flying level with ground

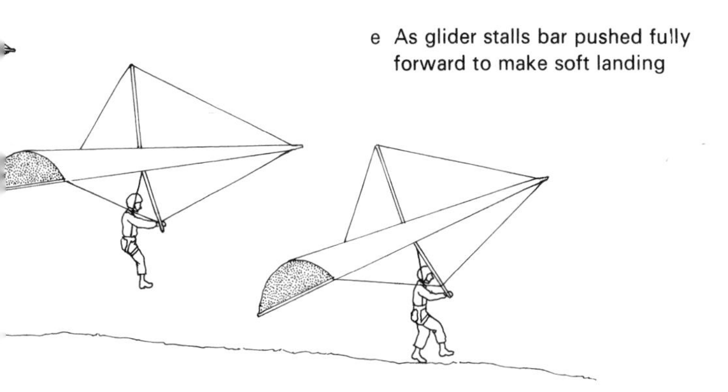

e As glider stalls bar pushed fully forward to make soft landing

so that when the aircraft stalls you have pushed the bar as far forward as you can reach. You will thus reduce the forward speed to nothing, if you have judged it correctly, so that you land lightly on both feet, with no forward motion at all.

Do not pull up your undercarriage when landing.

Touch Down Many pupils instinctively lift their legs as the ground comes up to them. Legs are designed for landing. If you pull them up out of the way, you will land on your buttocks, which are not designed for landing, and you may fracture your pelvis or spine. Your legs have built-in shock absorbers, so let them hang down to hit the ground first.

Pilots flying prone sometimes leave their preparations for landing too late and hit the ground while still in the prone position. The front of the chest and abdomen are not well protected, and if the ground is frozen hard or if you happen to hit a half buried rock or stump, or a piece of barbed wire you may be badly hurt. Even if there are no obstructions, or the ground is soft, you can easily damage your lungs, spine or abdominal organs in a hard landing.

OVERSHOOT AND UNDERSHOOT

If the field in which you intend to land is some distance ahead, you will want to be able to judge whether or not you can reach it. There is an easy way to do this. Choose some object on the downwind boundary: a bush, hedge, small building or post will do. Watch to see whether the top of it appears to be moving upwards into the landing field or downwards out of it, or whether the relationship stays constant. If the object appears not to move, you will land in the field just where you expect to (Figure 12a). If the object is moving down out of the field, you will land further into the field than you intended (Figure 12b) and you may even overshoot a small field. In this case make an S turn to lose some height (see page 56). If the object is moving up into the field, you are undershooting and will not reach the field (Figure 12c). If this is the case, never try to stretch your glide by flattening the glide path. You will lose height faster as you 'mush down' just before the stall; or you may even stall much too high and crash, or hit the fence on the boundary. For this reason check that there is somewhere safe to land on the way down. Recognise that you will not reach the field and make the best landing you can in whatever is underneath. A stall at 60 feet from trying to stretch your glide may result in a crash.

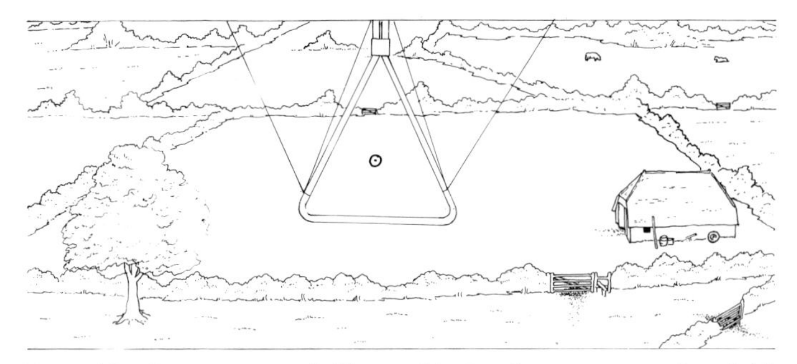

Figure 12a Correct approach. Tree and hedge do not move up into field: pilot lands on spot

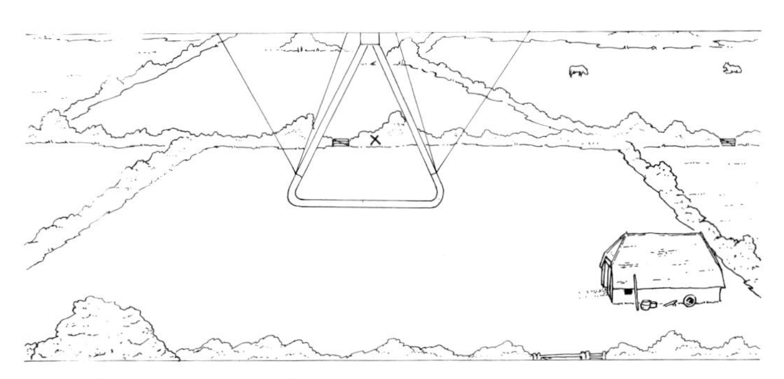

Figure 12b Overshooting. Tree and hedge have moved down out of field: aircraft will not come down before reaching far side of field to land at X

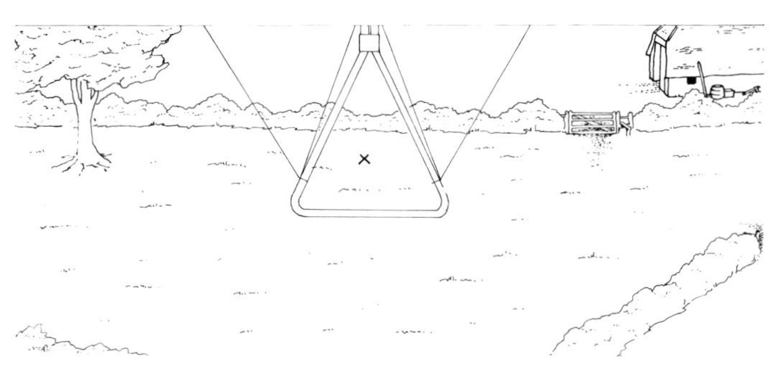

Figure 12c Undershooting. Tree has moved up into field, hedge has moved up to cover building: aircraft fails to reach field, lands at X

Pilot has pushed out bar too late and pulled up his feet. His legs are crossed.

DRIFT/SLIP AND SKID

As you make your approach to land, the ground should appear to be passing directly under your feet from front to back. If it is passing under you obliquely you must change the direction of your approach or you will land moving sideways as well as forwards, which has two disadvantages:

1 You will touch down at a faster speed than necessary because your line of flight does not give you the minimum ground speed.
2 You are more likely to twist your knee or ankle joints, or simply be thrown off balance, as you land. The aircraft may also be damaged.

If you are flying at your normal airspeed with the aircraft wings level, neither banked and slipping towards the centre of a turn, nor skidding away from the centre of a turn, your diagonal path is due to drift. It is caused by not flying directly into wind. To correct the drift, turn the nose of the aircraft directly into the wind. The aircraft will stop drifting immediately.

If, on the other hand, you are flying directly into wind but still appear to be drifting, you must be either slipping or skidding. This may well be because you have just made a late turn and not levelled up properly afterwards. Take off the bank if you are slipping in (Figure 13a), or increase the bank briefly if you are skidding (Figure 13b). How do you know which to do? The wind blowing on your face, together with the position of the wing, will tell you.

Be careful here. If you are heading a long way out of wind and accidentally turn the wrong way, you will be turning downwind. Your drift will disappear when you are flying straight downwind but you will be flying very fast over the ground. If you are too close to the ground to turn again, your best chance is to push out the bar as

Pilot at touchdown—glider stalled

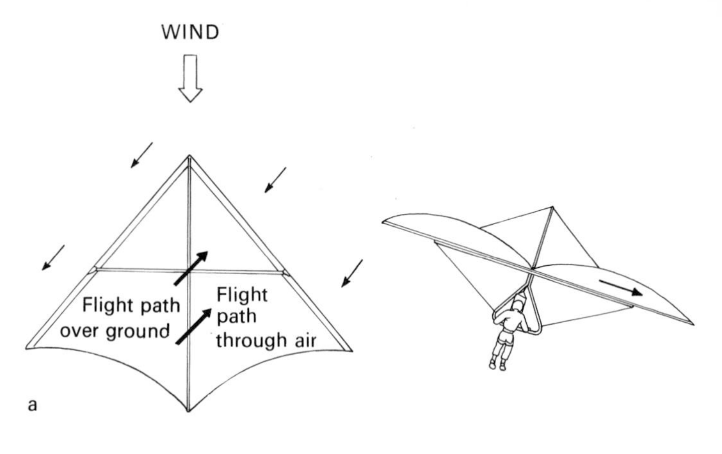

Figure 13 Slipping and skidding
Glider slipping to right. Wind felt on right side of face. Right wing down–bring glider level to check slip by moving to left

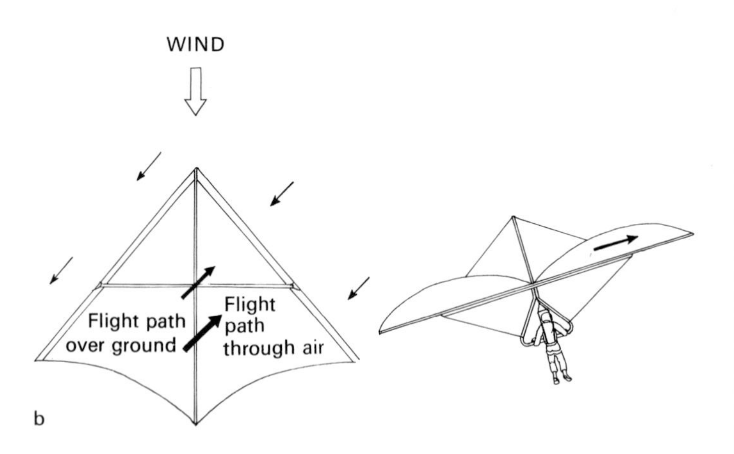

Glider skidding to right from flat turn, too late, too low. Centrifugal force throws pilot right. Wind felt on right side of face. Right wing up. Bank more to left to check skid, then level wings hard as possible just before you touch down: you will still hit the ground at the speed of the wind. A downwind landing is very hazardous and the greatest care should be taken to avoid one.

PARACHUTING

It may happen that, owing to lack of concentration or an unexpected lull in the wind, you will accidentally stall too high, perhaps at about 10 ft. This is too low to make a proper recovery: with little or no airspeed, you cannot make the glider fly. Remember that your glider is almost as big as a parachute and will behave like one, and slow your rate of descent. Hold the bar where it is as you come down.

A pilot will sometimes deliberately stall high and 'parachute down', either to land exactly where he chooses or else to avoid landing in a nasty place. It does, however, require considerable skill to do this properly, and many control bars have been bent in the process, because the landing will always be harder than normal.

5 The Flight Down

As your skill increases and you take off higher up the hill you will find that the gap between take off and landing gets longer; in this interval you are really flying. That, of course, is what you are there for – so let us now consider a few further aspects of technique.

CONTROL OF SPEED

As shown on page 15, your airspeed depends on the angle of attack. As long as you hold the control bar at a fixed distance from your body, your airspeed will remain constant. Altering the position of the bar, fore and aft alters your speed, and therefore the attitude of the glider, the glide angle and speed of descent. Remember, *the bar controls your speed* (Figure 14).

'SOUNDS' OF FLIGHT

Now if you listen, you will hear the sound of the air passing over your aircraft and, in many flexwing gliders, a fluttering of the sail. In a high performance glider with a well cut sail, there may be very little sound. These 'sounds' can be very helpful, although you are unlikely to notice them until you have made about six flights. The faster you go, the more wind noise there is. As you slow down, the noise becomes much less, and completely disappears just before the stall. If, when you are flying,

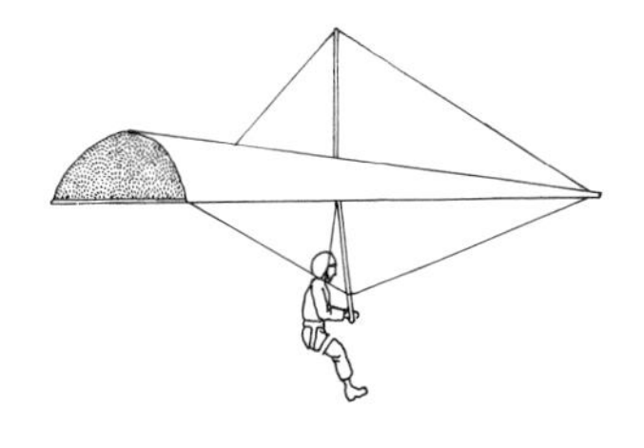

a Steady glide

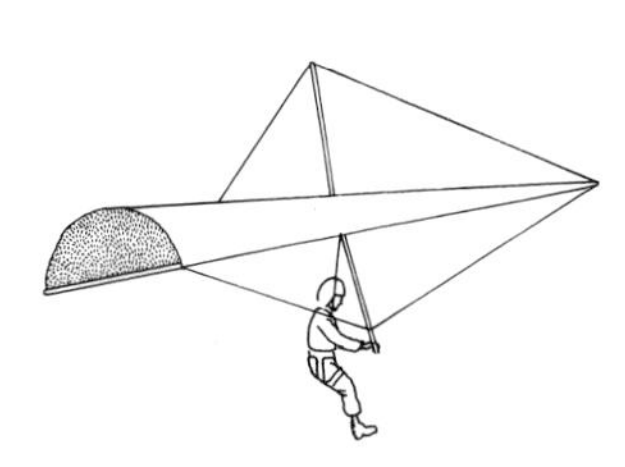

b Push on bar and nose goes up. Speed drops and rate of sink will also be reduced until speed falls to mushing point just before stall, when rate of sink will increase rapidly

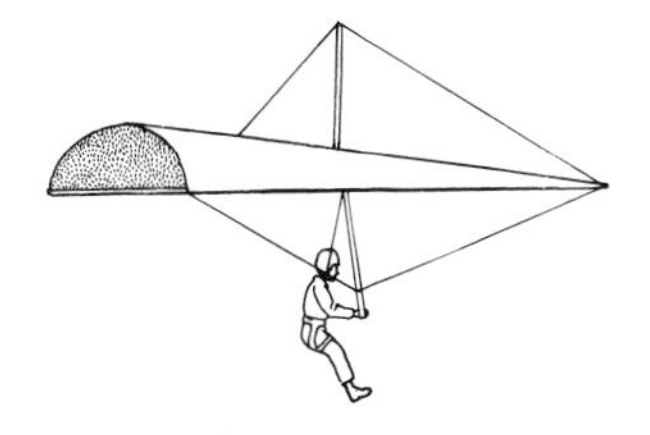

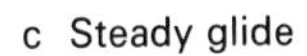

c Steady glide

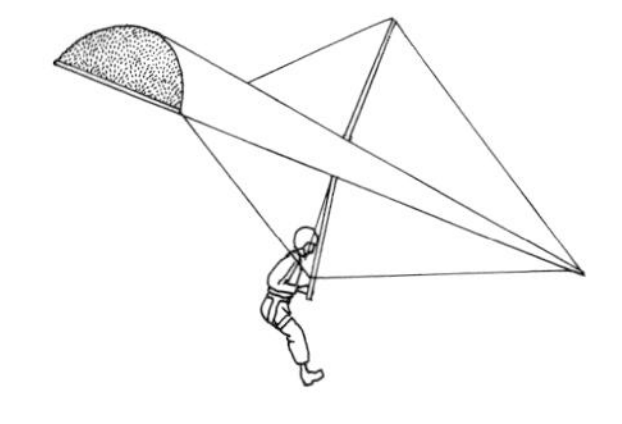

d Pull on bar, extend legs and nose goes down. Speed increases; as speed builds up, lift will increase and slow initial increased rate of descent. Nose will also start to rise

Figure 14 Speed control

you notice that everything has gone very quiet, pull in the bar a little to prevent a stall. Once you are accustomed to your normal flying 'attitude', and the sounds made by your aircraft in flight, you will instinctively notice any variations from this neutral position, when they occur.

STALLING

The ability to recognise and recover from a stall, and more particularly an incipient stall, is so important

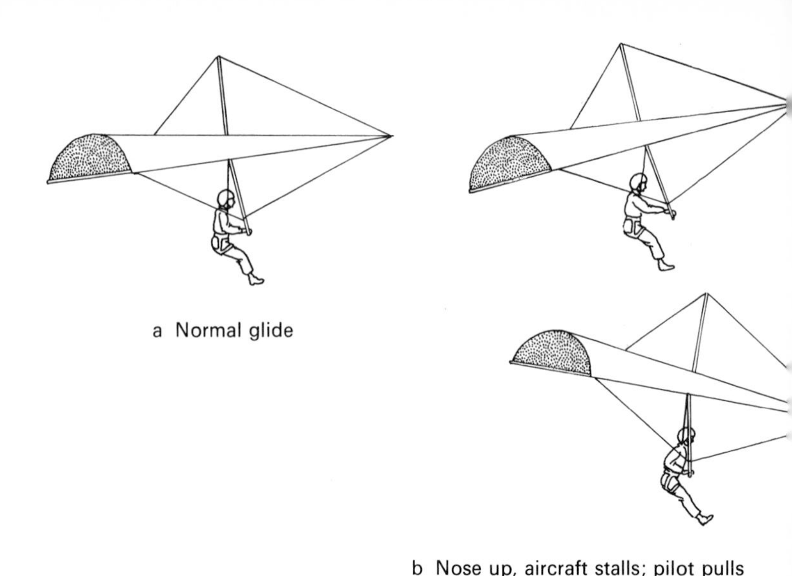

a Normal glide

b Nose up, aircraft stalls; pilot pulls bar to dive and increase speed

Figure 15 Stall
Speed too slow to keep airflow close to wing. Air breaks away and turbulence destroys lift

that it is part of every pilot's training. It is not part of the elementary certificate qualifications, because until you have made about 15 simple flights, and understand how the aircraft is controlled, it is unwise to experiment with stalling which, to begin with, is a little frightening. In any case you will not be flying high enough in the early stages for safe practice. However, as you may stall accidentally, you should know what to do.

When the aircraft stalls, it will lose height. How much height is lost depends on the type of aircraft, how much load the wings are carrying, the angle of attack and how quickly recovery is started. If the nose is very high, it will have to rotate downwards further before the dive necessary to build up speed again can begin: the aircraft will thus

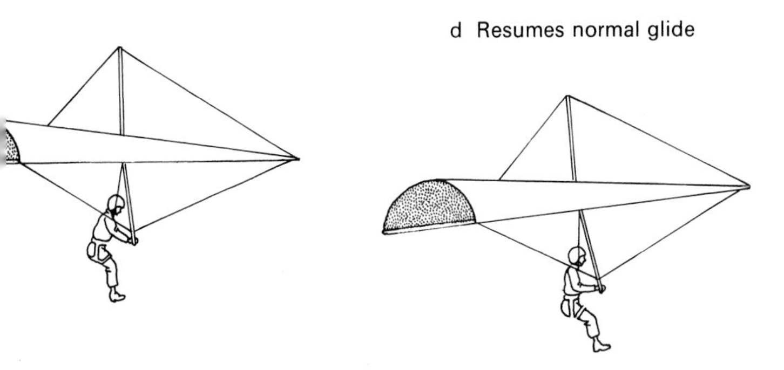

c Pilot eases bar forward to recover from dive

d Resumes normal glide

lose more height than if it had stalled in almost level flight. A simple low speed stall need cause very little loss of height, but it is wiser to assume that you may lose 50 ft or more, especially if you are stalling for the first time.

When you take off to make your first practice stall, give yourself about 200 ft or more of height above the ground. Glide straight down in your normal flying attitude, then apply gentle pressure to the bar to level your glide. Continue to apply pressure and you will notice that the normal flight noises become less, until they disappear altogether. At the same time, your rate of sink will increase noticeably and then the nose will drop. As soon as this happens, pull in the bar.

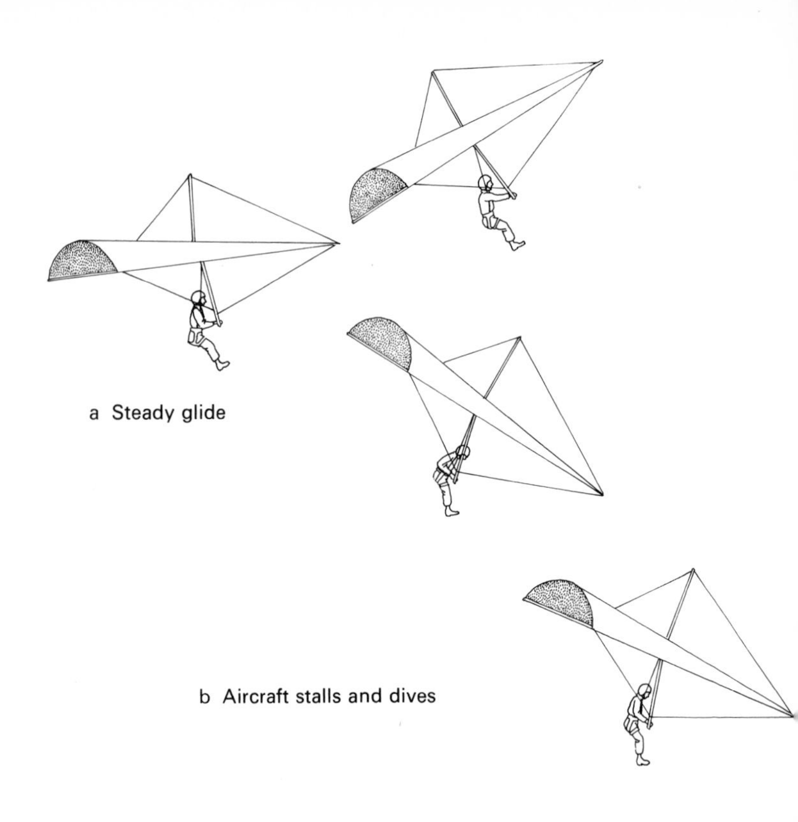

Figure 16 Stall, nose high. Stalling with the nose high results in a big change of attitude and loss of height. The aircraft falls and dives steeply before regaining flying speed. Aircraft rapidly goes up again in recovery, and will stall again if not checked

After pulling in the bar, you will feel that you are really falling, because there is a time lag before the aircraft responds to your actions. You are diving and gaining speed. As the aircraft picks up speed in the dive, your control will return, as will the flight noises, and you can again push on the bar to resume your normal glide.

Since you are now going faster than usual the aircraft will respond to your actions more rapidly, once it starts

c Recovery from dive

d Resumes normal glide

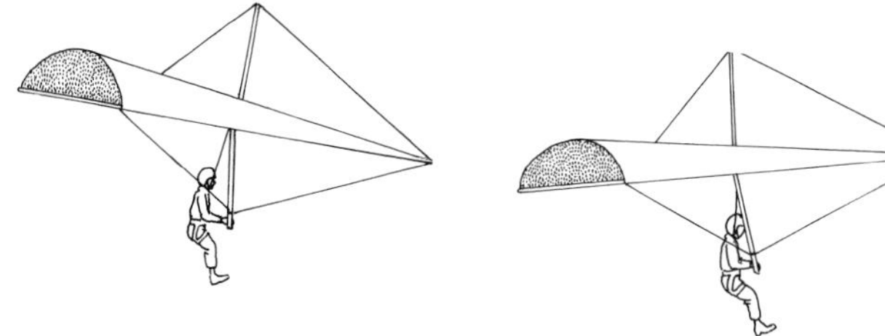

to move. Be ready for this response: do not zoom up too far and stall again by accident. The second stall will be more violent than the first and the loss of height greater, although the recovery procedure is exactly the same.

One word of warning: always look around and below before you stall, in case another glider is about to fly underneath you. If at any time you feel nervous while going into the stall and change your mind about it, you can prevent it by pulling gently on the bar to increase

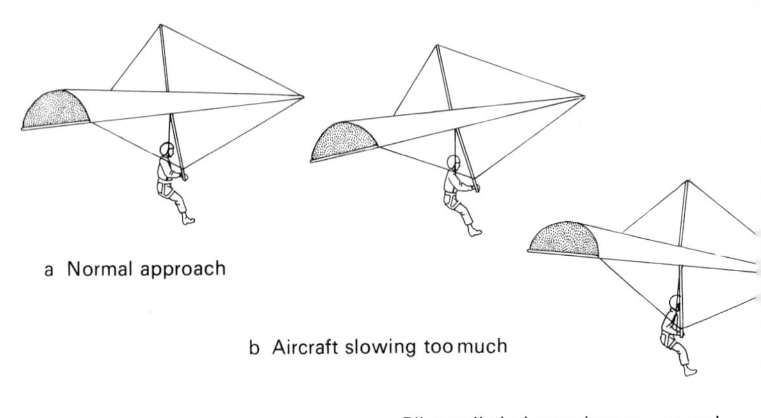

Figure 17 Incipient stall on approach

your speed. You can then begin again if you still have enough height.

The same technique is used if you forget the wind gradient (see page 34), and you accidentally allow your speed to drop too low when approaching to land. Quickly pull in the bar a fraction to pick up a little speed, then resume your normal approach.

TURNS

The next manoeuvre to be considered is the turn. Because the hang glider is a weight-shift aircraft and you are flying seated, if you point your feet to where you wish to go, the aircraft will turn and take you there. Straighten up when you are on the correct heading.

d Normal flare out

e Pilot pushes out bar for normal landing

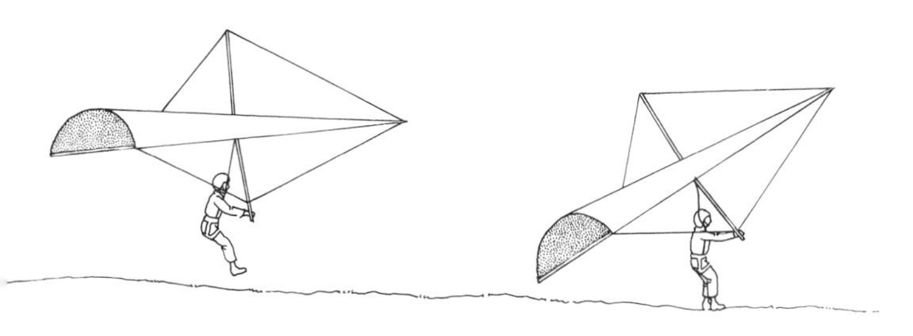

90° Turn For anything more than slight changes of course on your flight down, however, more complex action is needed. To begin with, you should learn how to make a 90° turn. Imagine that the wing is a large saucer; use the bar to tilt the saucer the way you want to go. Remember it like this:

1 Look out to one side at 90° and pick a landmark to turn on to; a cloud will do if the ground is bare. Also check that no other aircraft are in the way, or just behind you.
2 The stalling speed in a turn is higher than in a straight glide, so pull in the bar a little to increase your speed. This will also increase your rate of descent.
3 *At the same time*, bank the way you want to go–20°–30° will be enough. You will now be going slightly faster and slipping to one side with the nose going down.

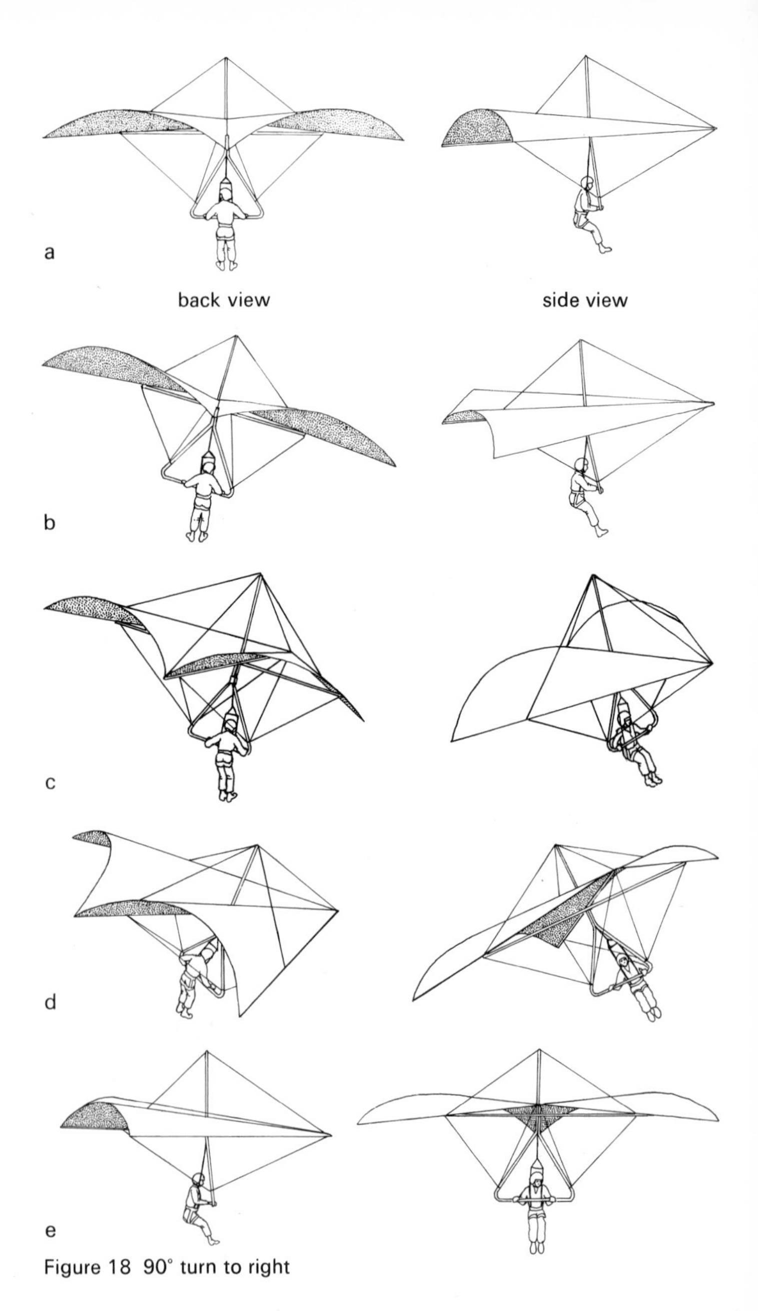

Figure 18 90° turn to right

4 *You must now push the bar slightly forward*, to push the nose round the turn, taking care not to stall as centrifugal force increases. (Figure 18b). If you do not do this, you will eventually point the way you want, but you will be diving and losing height. A turn should be made without losing very much more height than the straight glide, as the centrifugal force helps to hold the aircraft up.
5 Hold the aircraft in the turn until the nose has reached the landmark, then take off the bank and level the wings to resume the normal gliding attitude (Figure 18d).
6 Pull slightly on the bar to lower the nose (Figure 18e). This is normally combined with the movement to take off bank, to give smooth coordination.

In short, the turn is made by a continuous arc-like movement of the arms, which consists of pull in, push sideways, push out and hold, followed by a reversal of the movement on completion of the turn.

180° Turn For a 180° turn, the initial procedure is the same. Look round for other aircraft and pick your landmark, then go into a turn as before. Because the inside wing is going more slowly than the outside wing, the outside wing gives more lift. Because the inside wing is travelling on a steeper glide path, however, it also gives more lift. The lift is no longer acting at right angles to the ground, but is still acting at right angles to the aircraft. As, therefore, only some of it is available to hold the aircraft up, the aircraft would lose height more rapidly were it not for the centrifugal force. The stalling speed will be higher. If the speed is not increased, therefore, the aircraft may stall and the inside wing, which is closer to the stalling angle, will stall first, causing the aircraft either to turn sharply in the direction in which it is already turning, or to go into a spin.

During a prolonged turn the pilot will need continually to make small adjustments to the angle of bank, and the position of the nose, to keep the aircraft flying smoothly.

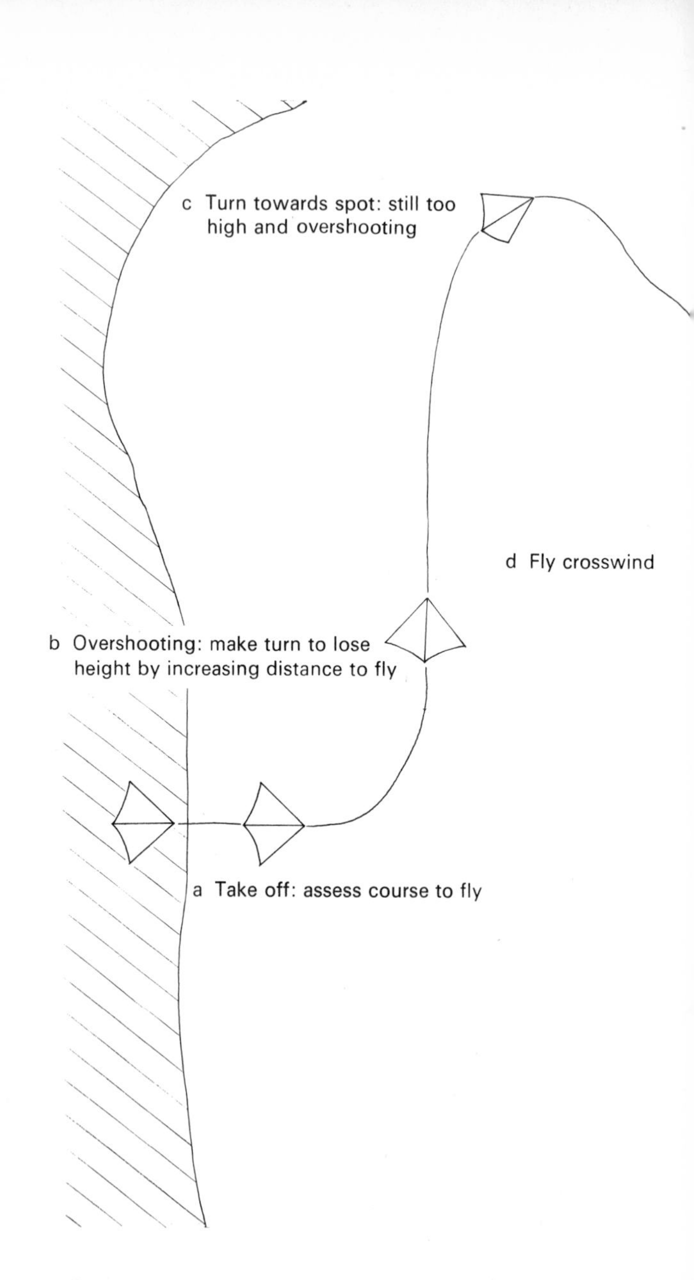

Figure 19 Spot landing

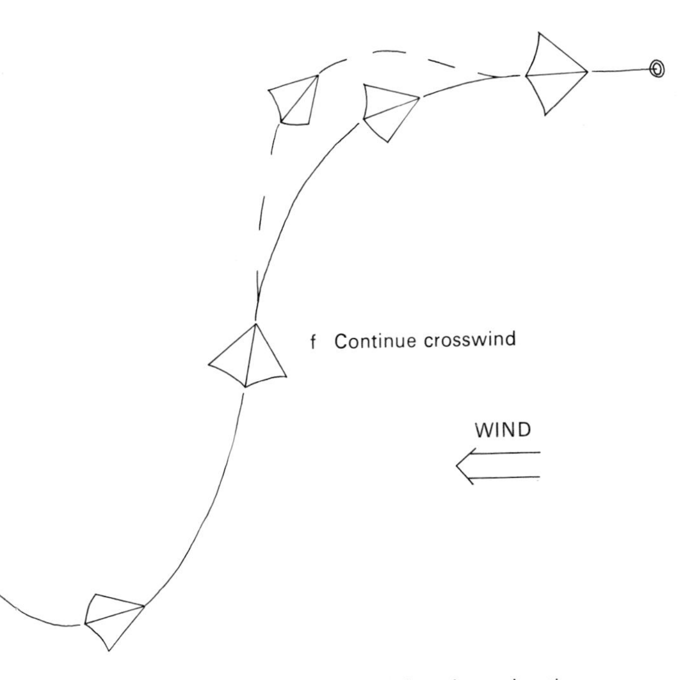
g Make final distance judgement, turn towards spot and land. Allow height for final turn
f Continue crosswind
WIND
e Turn towards spot: still too high and overshooting

The more steeply the aircraft is banked the higher the stalling speed will be. This applies high up or close to the ground. The pilot flying close to the ground cannot make a steep turn as the wing tip may touch the ground. If he turns sharply at slow speed the inside wing will stall. Turns near the ground must always be gentle.

S Turns You should now try to make S turns as you fly down. Take off, settle into your glide, turn right 90°, fly a short distance across wind, remembering to correct for drift by having the nose pointing slightly into wind, turn 90° left, then make your approach and land.

Do this on most flights now. As you begin to fly from higher hills, you will have more chance to make several turns on the way down, some of 180°, as you fly a 'beat' back and forth across the hill (see also page 59).

SPOT LANDING

You can now try to land on a predetermined spot. Before you take off, choose a spot on the field to aim for– an old motor tyre makes a good mark for this. Fly down making S turns, and try to land near the tyre. This is by no means as easy as you might think.

One word of caution: never make a bad landing trying to reach the spot. The most important thing is always to make a good landing. If you miss the spot, hard luck: make a better judged approach next time.

This practice will not only give you confidence in your ability to control the aircraft, but will also develop your skill in making good and accurate turns, which are necessary to achieve soaring flight.

6 Soaring

You can now take off, fly down smoothly and land just where you want to. The next big step forward is soaring flight. For this you will need a higher wind speed than you have flown in before, perhaps 14–18 mph. So don't rush it: work up to it gradually by doing the same things as before but in gradually increasing wind strengths in steps of 2–4 mph. This gives you not only plenty of practice, but also an opportunity to watch other flyers and see how it should be done.

CONDITIONS REQUIRED

The principle of soaring flight is this: the aircraft has a sink rate of a certain number of feet a minute and if you can find air which is rising faster than the aircraft is sinking, you can stay up.

Air rises due to a number of causes. The surest and easiest place to find rising air is where the wind is blowing straight on to the side of the hill: here the moving air hitting the sloping ground is forced upwards. The strength of the updraft depends on the speed of the wind, and the shape of the hill.

1 A long smooth ridge gives good lift to the air. A conical hill does not because much of the air can flow round it.
2 The slope must be fairly steep: a gradient of about 1 in 3 is good.

3 The wind must be steady: between about 14 and 18 mph is ideal.
4 The lift will depend on the surface terrain. A smooth slope will be better than one covered with ridges, rocks or bushes, which will slow down the air close to the ground and cause turbulence.
5 The terrain to windward will affect the wind, and the presence of another hill less than 500 yds to windward will upset the smooth flow of air up the hill.
6 A very steep hill or cliff will produce a strong lift band, but the area just below the edge and just behind it will be dangerous due to the rotors (circular movements of air) which always form in these locations.
7 There will be turbulence low down on the face of the hill and near to it.

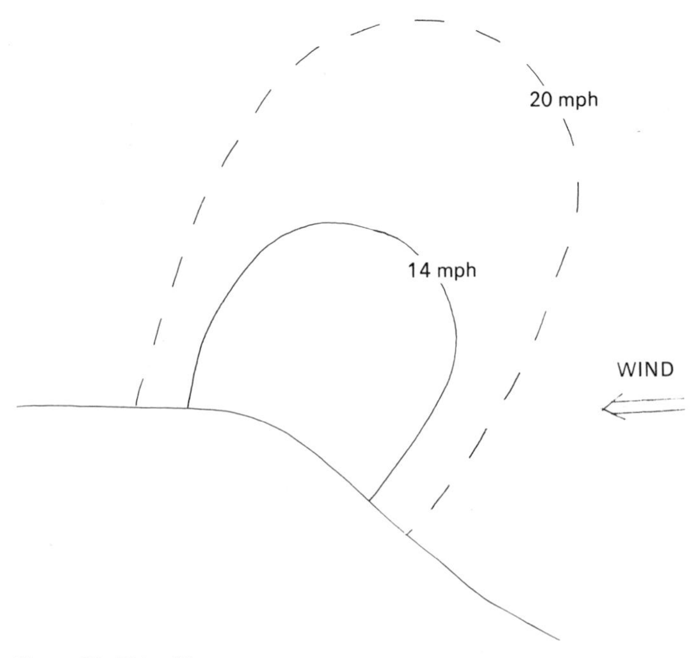

Figure 20 Ridge lift area
Area of lift extends at an angle of 45° approximately from just below crest of hill to windward. Stronger wind gives more lift

8 The lift band itself will be strongest on a line which extends out from just below the crest on the hill's windward side about 45° to the horizontal (Figure 20). Although narrow near the hill, the band will be wider as you fly higher in it. The lift also becomes weaker as you go up until at some point the lift will equal the sink rate of your aircraft, and that will be your 'ceiling'.

FLYING A 'BEAT'

In order to soar in the lift band, you must learn how to stay in it. This means that you must perfect your 180° turns until you can fly beats back and forth along the ridge and parallel to it. Practise with the wind perhaps about 12–14 mph, as shown in Figure 21. Do not come too close to the hill, or you will find yourself in the turbulent

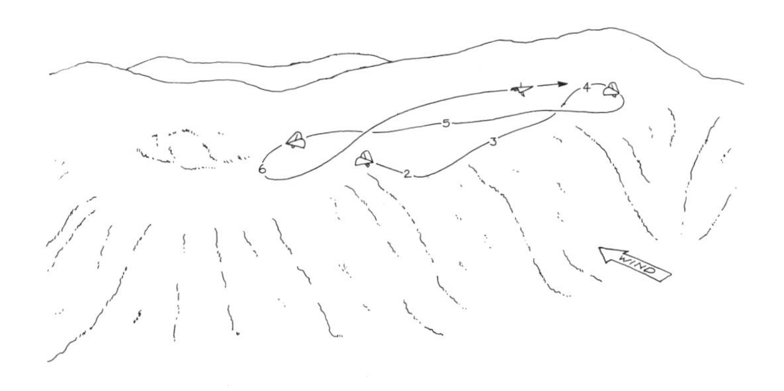

Figure 21 Beating the ridge
1 Take off
2 Turn quickly slightly to your left
3 Fly parallel to the ridge gaining height as the opportunity occurs
4 When you reach the end of the soaring area, turn right 180° *away from the hill*
5 Now fly along parallel to the ridge, but slightly higher and a little further out. You will pass your take off point
6 At the other end of the ridge, turn 180° *away from the hill,* to your left this time, and begin a new beat

air which is always to be found near the lower part of the face of the hill, and make an unexpected landing. When you are quite sure that you have mastered the turns you can try the real thing.

HOW TO SOAR

You will have to wait for a day with a smooth steady wind of 14–18 mph straight on to the hill, with no gusts exceeding 5 mph for more than 10 seconds. Get ready and take off in the usual way, but be ready for the lift–as your feet leave the ground you will be hauled up strongly, without the usual pause, as the aircraft goes into its glide. Pull in the bar a little more firmly than usual, and almost at once start a gentle turn to carry you crab-wise along the ridge. As you look round, the ridge should now be about 20–30 ft below and just a little behind and to one side. Stay in this position, as you fly along the ridge, drifting slightly to maintain your track across the wind. After a while you will reach the point where you have seen other flyers making their turns. As soon as you are ready, look round, then make a 180° turn *away from the hill,* levelling the wings when you are tracking back towards your take off point. You must make this turn smoothly and fairly tight, otherwise you will find you have flown out of the lift band on the windward side and lost a lot of height. If this happens, do not feel too disappointed; go down and land. A practised pilot may be able to work his way back into the lift, but if you try it yourself you will be more likely to crash on the hill side. You can always have another try if you have not bent a boom in a bad landing.

However, if you have made your turn correctly you will now be gliding back to your take off point, which you should pass a little higher than you left it. Carry on along the ridge to a turning point at the other end, then repeat the 180° turn always away from the hill.

On each beat you hope to gain a little height, until the lift equals the sink, and you have reached your ceiling.

As the wind is hardly ever completely steady, you will find that the amount of lift varies constantly. When you feel a gust hit the glider, ride it up by letting the bar out a fraction, exerting just enough pressure on it to maintain flying speed and penetration. When the wind drops and you feel a lull, pull in the bar a little, to prevent a stall, and try to stay in the lift band until the wind picks up. Do not try too hard–and if things begin to look a little risky, fly down and land.

HAZARDS

Shape of the Ground The lift is also very much affected by the shape and nature of the ground. Hill faces are not always flat but often have a series of alternating bays and spurs, causing gulley formations. Wind blowing straight into a gulley will give good lift in the middle, but less good lift at the sides. If the wind is blowing at an angle, it may produce a kind of whirlpool effect, which may cause your aircraft to stall and perhaps crash without warning. The lift will therefore vary; in some places you will begin to go down, in others the turbulence will make your flight a little rough.

Watch for a change of direction of the ridge; this will have a marked effect on the lift, which may increase or disappear altogether, so that you have to land. If there is a gap between two parts of a ridge where you can cross, make sure that you have enough height, and do not try this until you have plenty of experience. For this reason, always have a look at the ground before you fly over it.

Trees Trees will also cause turbulence, which will extend higher the stronger the wind, and give you a rough ride. If you fly too close to trees, you may hit a lull or a small rotor. On the windward side of a line of trees, however, there may well be a little welcome lift, to give you a small boost up when you thought all the lift had gone.

Soaring

Beginning the descent

Strong Wind When the wind is stronger, it is often better to take off a little lower down the face of the hill than usual, where the wind is less strong and will be blowing upwards rather than horizontally, making take off and penetration easier. You will find, however, that the wind may get under your tail and you will need to have the nose a little higher at take off to prevent too much sink. Remember to pull in the bar more quickly too.

Turbulence/Lull When you find yourself in a patch of turbulent air, fly a little faster. A sudden lull in the wind can pull your airspeed down to below stalling speed. At wind speeds below 10 mph, gusts are seldom strong enough to cause an accidental stall, but above 10 mph the possibility increases as the windspeed increases. This is especially dangerous if you are flying low over a clump of trees, or crossing a valley between two hills and have lost height, as you may then have insufficient height to recover.

Keeping a Look Out Remember always to keep a very good look out. Never turn without looking round first, and keep in mind where any other people are flying. Watch for other aircraft taking off after you. A glider below you probably cannot see you. A pilot making a turn will also have his view obstructed to some extent. You may have to turn away and lose the lift to avoid some nitwit who is flying badly. Never forget that it is your own life you are saving, as well as his.

7 The Wind

You must learn to see the wind. You must look at the country and try to see what the wind is doing, just as you would watch the water in a river flowing past obstacles, or the sea breaking over rocks. When you look at the ground from the top of a hill and see trees, buildings, hedges, haystacks or water, you must learn to see what the wind is doing as it moves over them.

DIRECTION

First of all, see which way the wind is blowing. Feel it on your face. Turn to face it, then turn to either side and determine the direction exactly. Pick a small handful of grass, throw it into the air, and watch what happens to it. Look down the hill and estimate the angle at which the wind strikes the face of the hill. Look for evidence of the wind direction in the landing area. There may be smoke, which is the best guide of all, unless it is coming from a moving ship or vehicle. Watch for thistledown blowing up the hill. There may be flags, which will show you the wind provided that they are not in the lee of a building or trees. A stretch of water will show 'wind lanes', streaks on the surface in the direction of the wind, which are usually very accurate. A field of wheat or corn will show ripples as the wind blows across it. Watch the birds. Seagulls, soaring, often remain stationary flying directly into wind at the same speed as the wind. Birds of prey such as hawks or kestrels do the same. Watch the birds landing: they always land into wind.

SPEED

Now estimate the speed. To do this you first need a *ventimeter* to give you the measured speed accurately. If you use it whenever you go flying, you will gradually learn to associate the feel of the wind on your face with the observed speed on the ventimeter. The sound made by the wind flapping the sail before you take off also tells you a good deal about the speed of the wind.

Feel the gusts and measure them carefully with the ventimeter. Measure the force of the gust above the average speed, and also how far below the average the wind speed falls in a lull. Measure also how long the gust lasts.

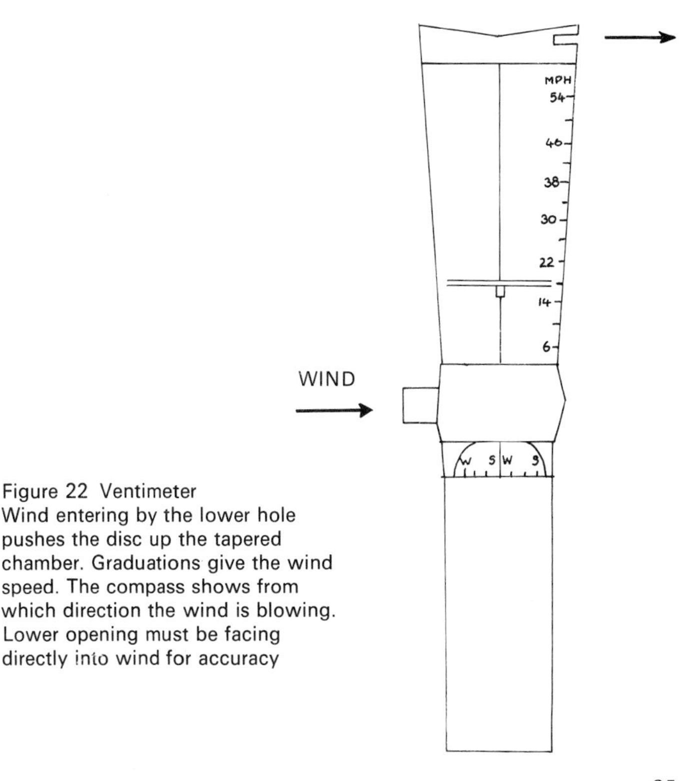

Figure 22 Ventimeter
Wind entering by the lower hole pushes the disc up the tapered chamber. Graduations give the wind speed. The compass shows from which direction the wind is blowing. Lower opening must be facing directly into wind for accuracy

EFFECT OF TERRAIN

Now look down on a collection of buildings, such as a farm. Think what will happen to a cloud of smoke as it is blown towards them. The smoke directly in line will be pushed up over the roof and billow upwards, perhaps as high again as the buildings or higher. After forming a crest the smoke will turn downwards and curl over like a breaking wave, but instead of going flat and turning into spray, the smoke will curl right under, going now in the opposite direction. It will then curl up again. Meeting the air coming over the building, it will be carried round to form a complete circle or a tube known as a rotor. Some of the smoke will billow out from the main breaking crest and go in other directions, showing the turbulence of the air. Leaves will be carried round with the smoke. Imagine yourself flying in that. You also are a leaf.

The smoke on either side does not rise up but curls round the sides of the buildings and comes in at the back and through the spaces between. To leeward or downwind of the buildings the turbulent air persists for a considerable distance, which might be equal to three or four times the height of the buildings. In stronger winds, these distances can be substantially increased and the highest point of the disturbance also moves downwind. Even a 5 ft high hedge will cause an area of turbulence for 15–20 ft to leeward. When you fly therefore, you must learn to avoid these places and not be surprised at the turbulence you will find if you venture in.

The wind blowing over the ground is slowed by friction. Imagine the smoke blowing along the ground. The lower layer will be rolling and swirling. Above this, the air will be moving faster and overtaking this layer and the smoke will be undulating only slightly. Higher still, the smoke will be moving even faster and parallel to the ground. You will actually be able to see the wind gradient.

As the smoke hits the foot of the slope, some of it will bounce back and as it hits the still onrushing air behind,

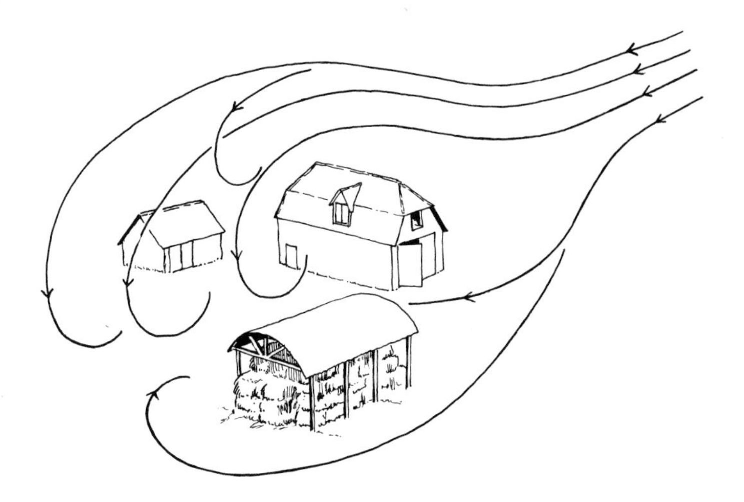

Figure 23 Smoke flowing over buildings

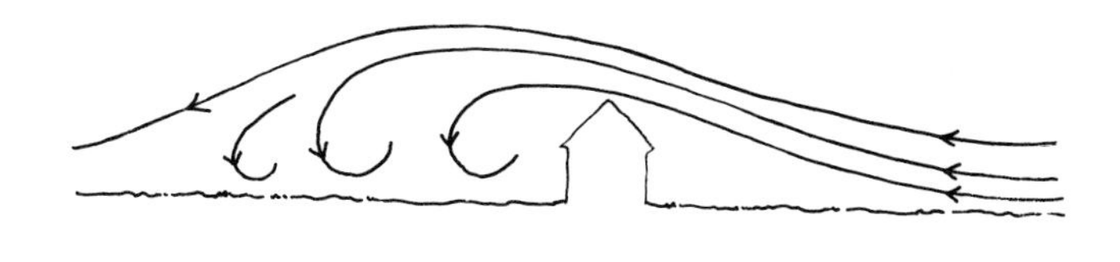

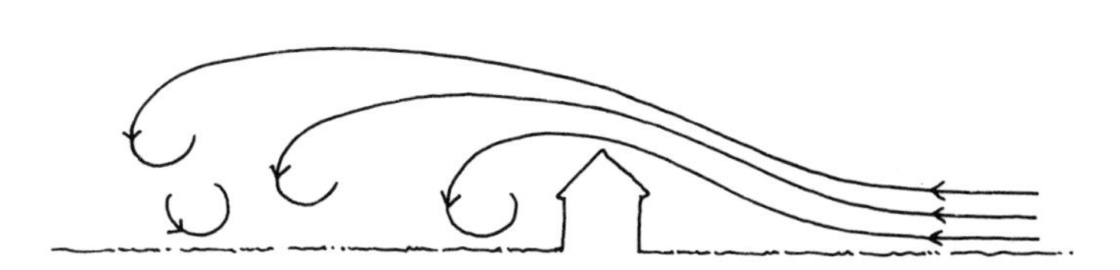

Figure 24 Strong wind causes turbulence to extend higher and further downwind of obstruction

be pushed up with it. The smoke puffs up vertically, leaving a boiling mass of air at the bottom and is immediately plastered on to the face of the hill again by the wind. It has now changed direction and is rushing up the hill. The wind gradient is still there but at right angles to the hill face. As it reaches the top it passes your take off point. As you stand and look out into wind therefore, you must learn to see what is in front of you:

1 A thin layer of the slower moving air immediately in front of you, moving upwards.
2 A little further out, air rising more strongly.
3 Above you, the air curling over and blowing back over your head.

If you follow the wind back, it flattens out to become horizontal over the crest of the hill, and then curls over again just behind the top in the same way as it did over the farm buildings to form another rotor.

Suppose now that at the bottom of the hill is a small spinney. As the smoke hits this, most of it will be forced up over the top, though some will pass between the trees. There will be a very small area of lift just in front of the trees. For a variable height above the trees however, the smoke will be billowing and turbulent, perhaps for 20 to 50 ft over the tops. It is dangerous to fly too close to trees. You may easily stall and land in the tops. This is the 'wood magnetism' you may have heard about.

Where else should you look at the wind? Let your gaze wander along the ridge on which you are standing. Where the wind blows straight on to the hill at 90°, it is deflected straight up and gives lift. Further along, the ridge may curve back away from the wind. What happens to the wind then? As the wind hits the spur, if follows it round and blows obliquely on to the hill face, not being forced upwards, and giving very little lift at all. If you fly out of your lift band and into this, you will lose height rapidly and soon be in the turbulent air near the hill face.

Further along still, the ridge may curve forwards again into wind and here the onrushing wind will be gathered up into a whirlpool and hurled upwards out of the bowl-like shape of the hill face. There will be lift but the down-currents will be just as strong as the up-currents, and the wind direction will be spiralling and very variable. Try to see what the wind is doing in this place and keep away.

There may be places where the shape becomes steeper, perhaps falling away to a cliff edge above the sea or a quarry. Imagine the smoke here hitting the edge. It will billow straight up to show very strong lift, curling down on to the top again just a little behind the lip. Below the lip the air will form rotors as it does a few feet behind the lip on the top. Stand near the edge of a cliff on a windy day and you will feel little wind. Throw out a small clump of grass and it will be picked up and hurled skywards. The same would happen to your glider if you ran off the edge. If you made a mistake, you would end up in the swirling air lower down.

Now walk backwards away from the edge and you will feel the wind coming from behind as you face the edge. What does this mean? Just that although you could take off from a cliff, to land there would be dangerous, as you would have to fly in the rotor, which would throw you down. You must therefore land either at the bottom well away from the cliff, so you may be in the sea if the tide is in, or well back behind the top where the air is smooth.

CROSS-WIND

If the wind is not blowing straight on to your take off point but hitting the hill obliquely, even as little as 10°–20° away from your take off run, the position is much the same as if you fly along over a place where the ridge turns away from the wind. The wind no longer comes up the hill but swirls along the face of the hill with much less of it moving upwards.

If there is another hill of comparable size less than 500 yds to windward, the wind between the two will be so turbulent as to be unsafe in anything over 10 mph. Take

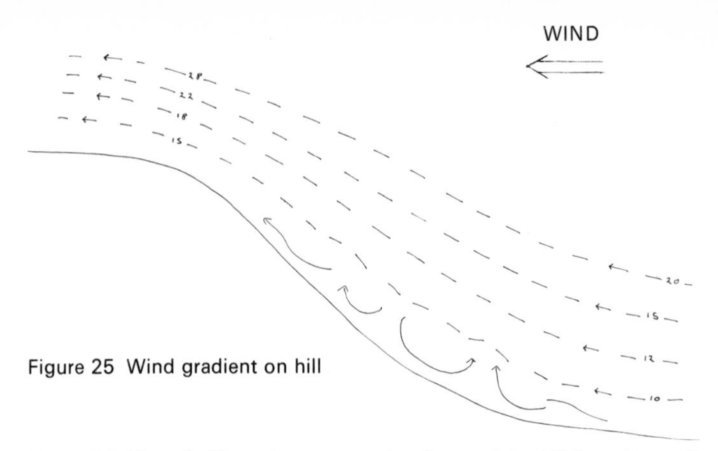

Figure 25 Wind gradient on hill

Figure 26 The windflow depends on the shape of the hill face. You will find it to be turbulent near cliffs, and smooth on rounded surfaces. There is greater lift on steep parts, and little lift on cross wind slopes

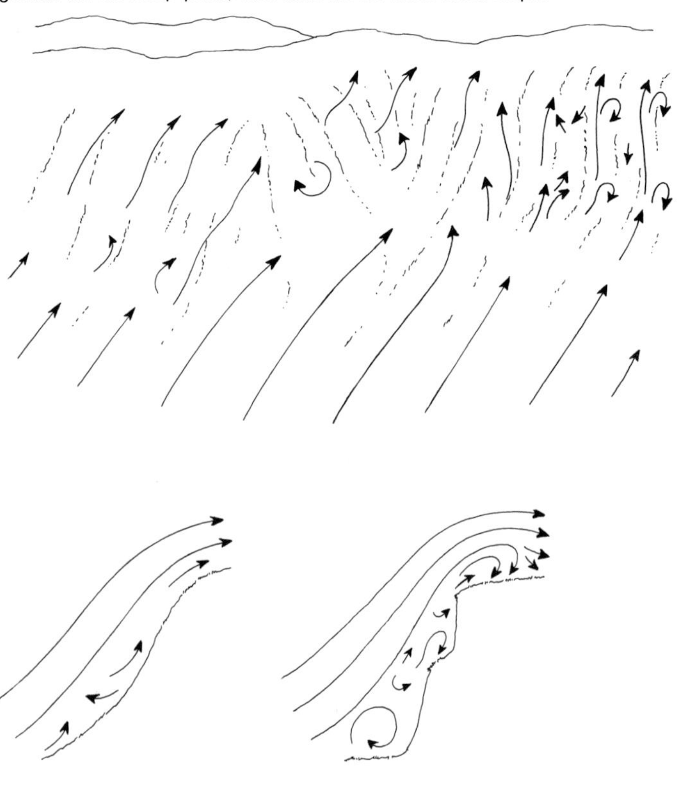

off will be satisfactory, but once below this level the wind will become very disturbed and landing at the bottom extremely hazardous. When a hill looks good to fly from, with a good take off area and a nice clear landing zone, do not be tempted if there is another hill directly upwind. The bigger the hill upwind, the further its influence will extend. You can be sure that in anything over a 5–10 mph wind you will be thrown about like a leaf in an alleyway.

THERMALS

Sometimes a bubble of air, warmer than the rest, will form and rise up through the cooler air. This is known as a thermal. Thermals frequently form over a ploughed field or a paved or built up area and drift downwind as they rise. You can only guess when they will form but they may drift up the hill. If you fly into one you will feel a sudden surge of lift, which carries you up faster, until you fly out of the other side. You feel a jolt as you pass into the descending air at the edge before resuming your flight in the main airstream. When you have more experience and can make a 360° turn, you can use these thermal bubbles to gain height (see chapter 8, page 75). For the present just try to imagine what they are like.

NOTES ON WIND

At the slow speed at which a hang glider flies, the wind becomes very important, especially near the ground. Air flows smoothly over shapes which do not require a large change of direction but breaks away when the deflection is large. At wind speeds in excess of 10 mph, a hang glider may stall simply because of a sudden lull in the wind.

A few observations may be of help–

1 Air coming in from the sea tends to be smooth, with fewer gusts than over land.

2 When the wind gradient is large, as over a very rough surface or when warm weather is causing many

thermals, the landing approach should always be made with extra speed.

3 Avoid flying in the lee of anything which will disturb the wind flow.

4 In turbulent conditions, the shocks felt by the pilot and the glider will be more severe at high speeds.

5 In a valley, the wind blows up the slope in the day time and downwards in the evening, due to convection. It is stronger on the sunny side, unless the prevailing wind over-rides the local air movement.

6 As you fly higher, the wind veers (direction moves clockwise) and becomes stronger (the opposite applies in the southern hemisphere).

7 Strengthening surface wind veers, slackening surface wind backs (direction changes anticlockwise). The opposite applies in the southern hemisphere.

8 What Next?

You have now learnt how to fly a hang glider. You are a beginner on the threshold of an exciting sport. Your total flying time so far will probably be, at most, about half an hour. This book does not aim to teach you any more, but you should know a little about what lies ahead.

TOP LANDING

When you have acquired sufficient skill at soaring and controlling the flight of the glider, you will be able to learn how to land back on the top of the hill instead of flying to the bottom and walking up. To do this you have to fly the glider behind the take off point, where the lift is very much less, without going so far back as to fly into the rotor over the top of the hill. If you do not fly far enough back, you cannot lose enough height to land before you are again caught up in the lift band. You must learn to fly back to arrive at a specific point, descending slowly with airspeed matching wind speed, so that you come down almost vertically over your selected landing spot. The technique for doing this varies with every hill and depends also on the wind speed and direction. For this reason, top landing is not always possible on every hill under all wind conditions. When you are ready to learn, watch other pilots doing it and ask them to describe how it is done. If you make a mistake, fly off and try again; do not come in determined to land regardless of the

Flying prone

Pilot pushing out bar to slow descent and reduce speed

consequences or you will almost certainly need a new control bar.

360° TURNS

More pilots have had bad accidents doing 360° turns than performing any other manoeuvre. This is because many, not taking the trouble to understand the aerodynamics involved, have lost control and crashed.

Why does anyone do 360° turns anyway? There are several reasons. During a long descent, a pilot may wish to remain over the place where he intends to land rather than fly away and come back to it. The terrain, except for the landing area, may be unsuitable for a landing or have dangerous wind currents. By circling over his landing spot he can be sure of a safe descent.

When he has sufficient skill to fly cross country, he will need to circle in a thermal to gain height. In the same way, a pilot flying in the ridge lift must circle within the band of rising air before setting off to fly to the next ridge or to look for thermals.

Making good, safe 360° turns, without losing height unintentionally, requires skilful flying which your instructor will explain to you. You must also have at least 500 ft of height for safe practice.

USING A 'VARIOMETER'

A thermal may be large or small. It may rise only a few hundred feet before it disappears into air at the same temperature, or it may rise for tens of thousands of feet in a cumulus cloud system. Glider pilots look for and use thermals to gain height for cross country flying (see page 76).

To find them, and stay in them, an instrument called a *variometer* is needed. A variometer measures changing air pressure. It consists of a pressure gauge, connected to an indicator, which tells the pilot whether the air in which he is flying is rising or falling.

This means that when the glider flies into a thermal, the change of pressure will instantly be picked up by the variometer and shown as lift. The pilot then has to fly his glider to keep the lift registering on the variometer. When the lift disappears, he makes a guess as to whether to turn left or right to re-enter the thermal. If he guesses correctly, the variometer will again start to record the rising air, which is taking the glider up.

HIGH FLYING

The skilful pilot, flying a good glider, is able to gain a lot of height by using thermals. In fact it is possible for him to exceed 10,000 ft and this kind of flying brings with it another group of hazards. Cold and lack of oxygen are the principle ones. The temperature falls approximately 2°C for every thousand feet gained in height. From 15°C at sea level therefore, at 8000 ft the temperature has dropped to below freezing. The high flying pilot needs warm clothes, gloves and boots. As the pressure decreases with the increase in height, the amount of oxygen which the body can take from the air becomes less. This has the effect of making the pilot short of breath and deprives his brain of oxygen, so that his reason is disturbed and he behaves as if drunk. If he flies higher still, he loses consciousness. For any flying above 10,000 ft, a pilot needs extra oxygen in order to breathe.

CROSS COUNTRY FLYING

With a normal cruising speed of between 15 and 25 mph, cross country flying must be almost downwind. Nevertheless, providing that you are prepared to go where the wind goes, without a fixed destination, quite a long cross country flight is possible. This may be done by ridge soaring, that is, gaining height and flying along the ridge until you reach the end and then, if you have sufficient height, flying across to the next ridge. In this way your progress will be across the wind direction, but will be limited by the extent of the ridge. A soarable ridge or series of ridges may extend for many miles, so that it is possible to travel a long way in the right wind conditions.

The other method is to use thermals. For this, a high performance glider is needed. The pilot takes off from a ridge, which need not be very high and then gains height until he can find a thermal. The first 3000 ft are the hardest, but once enough height has been gained, thermals will be easier to find and use, and because the wind usually becomes stronger higher up, distance covered over the ground will be greater.

Sometimes a combination of methods can be used by 'riding' the thermals to fly from one ridge to the next. At times cross country flying also requires the pilot to read a map and use a compass. Map reading while flying a hang glider takes some practice, and most pilots will probably spend some time studying the map and planning a possible route before take off, if they do not know the country well beforehand.

PRONE FLYING

You will learn to fly initially in the seated position. After some practice, most people will wish to learn how to fly prone. The advantage of doing this is that the body presents a much smaller area to the slipstream in the horizontal position, so that the frontal area may be reduced by about two thirds. This cuts down the drag and improves the performance to such an extent that it may well make the difference between soaring and not soaring in marginal wind conditions.

There are, however, one or two hazards, which demand caution. The amount of control in the prone position is greater, for the pilot can put his weight much further forward than a seated pilot, who can only pull the bar back until it meets his body. This means that the prone pilot can go faster and dive more steeply. It also means that he is more likely to damage the aircraft by straining it. Learning to control the aircraft in the prone position takes time and a number of pilots have crashed soon after take off because they did not appreciate this fact. Losing control after gaining about 30–50 ft after take off is particularly dangerous, as the glider is likely to turn downwind and hit the hill at high speed after stalling.

There are a number of different types of prone harness. It is as well to examine several of them, and discuss their merits with the pilots who use them before buying one. Take off and landing are made in the usual way. The harness allows the pilot to swivel his body into the prone position, and the upright position is assumed again just before landing. Landing prone is never to be recommended; although it frequently occurs without mishap, the possibility of injury is high.

COMPETITIONS

For those who are interested in competition flying, hang gliding offers many opportunities, and a high degree of skill is required to win. In all competitions a good take off and landing are required if marks are not to be lost. The first two types of competition ever held were those where:

1 A pilot was asked to land on a designated spot.
2 A pilot was asked to fly the longest possible distance from a fixed take off point.

These two types of competition are still in operation, but there are now more difficult ones which take into account the increasing development and better performance of the gliders and the continually improving technique of the pilots. Nowadays a competition is likely to include the following events, in addition to the first two:

3 A pilot is asked to take off and fly a zig-zag or slalom-type course between pylons.
4 After take off, a pilot is required to fly through a 'gate', and then to remain in the air for as long as possible before finally landing on a given spot.

5 A pilot takes off and flies over a pylon. He then flies as slowly as he can to another pylon. He now turns and flies back over both pylons as fast as he can, before landing on a spot. Marks are given for passing accurately over the pylons, the difference in time between the two runs, and the landing.

Cross country competitions are likely to increase in popularity as the gliders are developed. Both distance flown and time over a set course are popular criteria.

Hang gliding competitions are held for the benefit of the participants, and most do not care whether anyone is watching or not. However, because of the beautiful and spectacular nature of hang glider flying, a crowd often forms and the competitions can be really entertaining to watch.

TOWING

The idea of towing a hang glider to achieve take off and gain height is attractive, especially if there are no hills in the district. However, towing can be extremely dangerous if incorrectly done. Only specially built hang gliders, with steel control frames, designed to withstand the additional strain of towing, are suitable. It should never be attempted except under instruction from a pilot who has considerable experience of towing.

BALLOON DROPS

Another means of gaining height is to attach the glider to a balloon (usually a hot-air balloon) and then release it at a suitable height. Using a balloon, a glider can be taken up to 20,000 ft or more: a hang glider has crossed the English Channel from Dover to Calais after being released at 18,000 ft from a balloon.

The air becomes very cold above 5,000 ft and the pilot must be suitably clothed. To fly down from 15,000 ft to sea level may take the best part of an hour, most of which will be spent at temperatures below freezing.

POWERED FLIGHT

A third answer to the problem of take off where there are no suitable hills, is to fit a small engine which will be powerful enough to enable the pilot to take off and climb to a reasonable height. Once in the air, the pilot can stop the engine and fly like any other glider.

Another advantage conferred by the engine is that, provided it can be started in flight, the pilot can use it to help himself out of a hazardous situation or perhaps to avoid the necessity for landing due to loss of lift. The speed attained by the aircraft is not likely to be any greater than it would be without the engine, so that, except on a calm day, the direction of travel would still be dictated by the wind. It is not likely that a hang glider would carry fuel for more than about half an hour because of the weight, though the engine itself need not weigh much and consumption will be low.

Before attempting to fly a powered hang glider, a pilot would have learned to fly without an engine, and have had a good deal of practice.

9 Safety Precautions

When a would-be pilot first sees a hang glider flying and decides that that is what he wants to do, he feels only joy at the prospect. When he actually clips himself to his glider and stands poised for take off, he may well feel only fear. This is a normal, healthy reaction, if the fear is moderate, and he understands what he is trying to do.

Flying is largely a matter of self confidence. As your skill improves and your self confidence increases, your flying will get better, improving until you can take off skilfully and cleanly, fly smoothly, and land with precision.

You must now beware of over confidence, which can prove to be very dangerous. It strikes even experienced pilots. Never be careless about your flying. Just because you have gained in skill and experience, your aircraft will not disobey the laws of aerodynamics. At stalling speed, it will stall. No pilot ever relies on getting a second chance. You should not feel afraid of flying but you must always keep a healthy fear of what will happen if you lack care.

There are a few other things you must know in order to live to a ripe old age.

ALCOHOL

Much flying is discussed over a drink. In the evening after flying there is no harm in this. During the day while waiting for the weather to improve, moderation is essential. No pilot should ever have more than one pint of beer or one tot of spirits if he intends to fly later in the day. It is better not to drink at all less than 12 hours before flying. So long as the immediate uplift of alcohol is still being felt, or the after effects of too much drinking are being experienced, a pilot should never fly.

MEDICINES AND DRUGS

Both the intended effects of medicines and drugs, and the side effects may make a person who is taking them unfit to fly. Ask the doctor or chemist who prescribes them for you whether it is safe to pilot an aircraft while using them. Sometimes, drugs react with each other or with alcohol to produce an exaggerated or even toxic effect. Sedatives and cold-cures are the most common types of medicines which may impair judgement.

EARS

Most of your flying in the early days will be from hills less than 500 ft high. When you start to fly higher, however, it is important to know something about your ears. The atmospheric pressure is maintained equally on both sides of the ear-drum by a small tube which runs from the middle ear to the back of the nose. As you climb the hill, atmospheric pressure decreases and air in the middle ear forces its way out through this tube to the nose. The ears will 'pop' about every 500 ft on the way up.

On the way down, the tube must be opened about every 1,000 ft to allow air back into the middle ear. The act of swallowing usually does this automatically, as does yawning. However, if descent is fairly rapid, as it may be while flying a hang glider, these natural methods may not be fast enough. It is then necessary to pinch the nose, and, keeping the mouth closed, blow hard. This will inflate the back of the nose and cause the valve to open, and a pop will be heard.

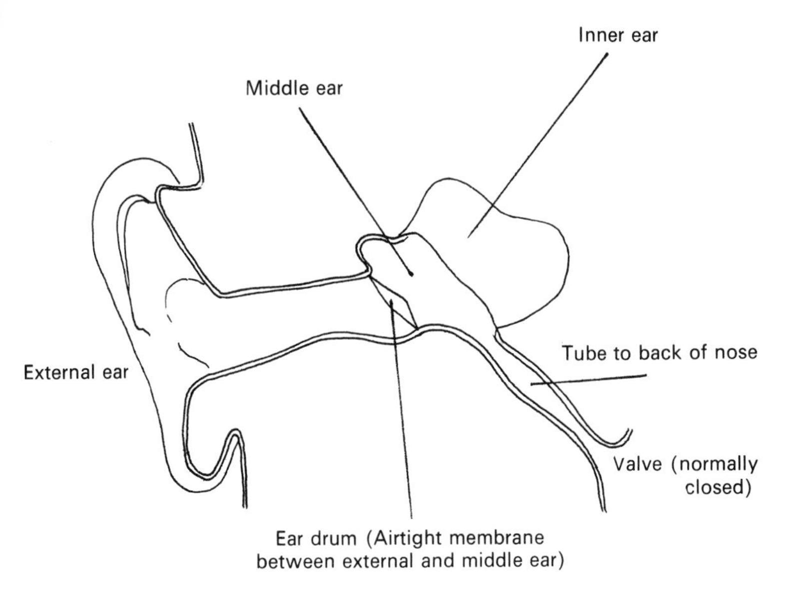

Figure 27 Structure of ear

If this is not done, the ear-drum will be pushed in by the increasing pressure outside. This will lead first to deafness, so that you no longer hear the wind noises, then to pain, severe pain and finally to rupture of the ear-drum with excruciating pain and probably severe giddiness, either of which would make control of the glider practically impossible.

Since the only way to reduce pressure on the ear is to go up again which you will probably be unable to do, you must clear the ears regularly on the way down. If you have a head cold and cannot clear your ears, never fly from higher than 500 ft.

CLOUDS–NOT FLYING IN THEM

Flying in a cloud without instruments is not possible. Anybody who doubts this should try the following experiment. Sit on a revolving seat and hold on to it. Close your eyes. Now either spin yourself round with your feet, or ask somebody else to turn you round to the left. After a few revolutions, the sensation of turning will become less, or even disappear altogether. After a few more revolutions, stop turning. Keeping your eyes closed, note that you now feel as if you were turning to the right. Now, with your head tilted backwards and your eyes closed, spin to the left again. When you stop spinning, lift your head upright. Be careful, you may fall off the seat to your right. You can try the same experiment with your head tilted forward or lying sideways on either shoulder, and turning to left or right. Each time you will have a different sensation. Even if you keep your eyes open, the sensation will still be very strong, and you will find it hard to believe your eyes. Even though you know that you are stationary, the room will appear to be spinning.

If instead of being seated on a stool you are flying, in addition to being able to move in rotation round three axes instead of one, you can also move up and down and to one or other side. You can also accelerate or slow down. All sensations due to these movements will be in addition to those caused by rotation. It must therefore be obvious that if you are flying in a cloud, or the visibility is so bad that there is no clear horizon, without instruments you cannot tell which way up you are or in which direction you are moving.

To fly in a cloud an aircraft needs the following instruments:

1 Airspeed indicator.
2 Altimeter.
3 Rate of climb and descent indicator, or variometer.
4 Artificial horizon.
5 Turn indicator.
6 Bank (slip or skid) indicator.
7 Gyro compass.

Any four of these instruments are sufficient as they give information which overlaps the other instruments to some extent, but nobody willingly flies in cloud without them all.

It is not safe therefore to fly in cloud in a hang glider, despite the fact that a hang glider is a fairly stable aircraft, and will probably fly straight if undisturbed by a gust of wind. Once upset, the equilibrium can only be restored by the use of instruments. It is quite possible to be out of control in less than 30 seconds after flying into a cloud. If you cannot see your landing field from your take off point because of fog, do not fly. Even if you do not lose control, you may still hit some other flyer or an obstacle hidden by the cloud. It is also illegal for a pilot not rated for instrument flying to fly in cloud.

PARACHUTES

The original Rogallo hang glider was very little better than a guided parachute, and was only flown in a ground-skimming way. As soon as it became possible to gain height, the idea of having a parachute in case of trouble seemed more attractive. After all, even parachutists carry a spare in case the first fails.

Being harnessed to the aircraft, the pilot of a hang glider has two choices. Either he can abandon the aircraft and use a parachute in the conventional way, or the parachute can be used to save the glider as well as the pilot. Since the glider only weighs about 50 lbs and the harness being used to fly the aircraft is strong enough, the second alternative seems more practical. It is of course also much quicker, since parting from the aircraft is not necessary.

Should the glider go out of control, it may be overstressed. This may cause structural failure. The pilot then deploys his parachute and makes a safe if undignified landing. The parachute may be anchored either to the pilot or to the glider and only adds another few pounds to the total weight.

INSURANCE

Insurance is important to you in a number of ways.

Third Party If you accidentally land on somebody's Rolls Royce, or fall through a greenhouse or break a spectator's leg, it may well cost you a lot of money. You may bring down a telephone wire or black out a village. A member of the BHGA is automatically insured for £250,000 for third party risks so long as he has not broken the rules. It is worthwhile joining the Association for this reason, if for no other, because the same insurance privately is likely to cost more. You cannot afford to be without it.

Personal Injury It may never happen to you of course, but if it does you will need insurance. For about £10 to £15 per year you can be insured for £10,000 against severe injuries. If you are injured, you may not be able to follow your occupation. For a further premium of £15 per year you are entitled to draw £30 a week for two years, except for the first 14 days.

Perhaps £30 a year for insurance seems rather a lot; yet it is a lot less than you pay to insure a car, and you do not need to buy fuel for a hang glider.

Existing Policies Policies taken out before you started flying a hang glider will probably not be affected, but if you take out a new one, your flying will have to be declared and a small loading will probably be added to the premium. If you are buying a house and have a mortgage, you should be insured to cover your flying.

Insurance for the Glider Insurance against the glider being damaged in a flying accident is not usually worth the premium required, but for a small charge the glider can be insured against damage sustained while it is on the ground, or on the roof of your car. The premium is about a third of the cost of replacing one of the main booms, if somebody should accidentally land on your parked glider and bend it.

The BHGA has an expert adviser on insurance. Every pilot should take the precaution of insuring himself–it is too late when you are in hospital.

10 Rules and Common Sense Measures

FLYING RULES

Look Round Never remain looking in one direction for more than a few seconds. Always be aware of the position and movement of other aircraft.

Turn Right When two aircraft are approaching each other head on, each shall alter course to the right. (Bear in mind that when close to a ridge at least one of the aircraft may have little room to manoeuvre – give way early.)

Give Way to Aircraft:

1 On your right.
2 Which are turning.
3 Which are below you.

Keep 100 Feet Apart When converging from any direction:

1 Slow your closing speed.
2 Turn away if necessary.

There are numerous other rules and regulations concerning aircraft. Once you move beyond the elementary stage of flying you must learn these rules and observe them. Here are a few of the ones you are most likely to encounter.

Flying Without Instruments A hang glider without special instruments, and whose pilot has not had special training, can only fly under visual flight rules (VFR).

These are simply:

1 Fly only when visibility is at least one nautical mile.
2 Fly only if clear of cloud and in sight of the earth's surface.

Flight Restrictions

1 A hang glider may not fly in controlled air space without permission.
2 A hang glider may not fly over towns below a height which would enable it to land clear of the area or below 1,500 ft above the highest fixed object within 2,000 ft. Nor shall it fly over or within 1,000 yds of any open air assembly of more than 1,000 persons, nor closer to any person, vessel, vehicle or structure than 500 ft except with permission in writing of the Minister of Aviation. Exemption exists for normal take off or landing or hill soaring.
3 The traffic zone of an air field is the airspace up to 2,000 ft above it and within one and a half nautical miles of its boundaries. A glider may not be flown into such zones without permission except for the purpose of landing. It must make all turns to the left and keep the manoeuvring area on its left unless directed otherwise, remaining clear of cloud and at least 500 ft above the field.

Accidents An accident which causes injury or substantial damage to an aircraft must be reported to the police and the Civil Aviation Authority, Accidents Investigation Branch (tel: 01-217 3627) and confirmed in writing. The aircraft must not be moved without the permission of the AIB other than to extricate the pilot, or to avoid damage by fire or danger to the public.

Extracts from the BHGA Code of Good Practice

1 Ensure that the permission of the landowner, occupier or controlling authority has been obtained before using a hill. This includes the landing area also, which may belong to a different person.

2 When visiting sites administered by clubs other than your own, always contact them in advance and observe their local rules.
3 Do not fly so as to interfere with farm animals especially when they are about to bear young.
4 Do not land in growing crops.
5 Use only recognised gates and paths.
6 Always close gates.
7 Do not climb over walls or fences, or through hedges.
8 Make sure take off and landing areas are free from spectators.
9 Do not leave a rigged glider unattended.
10 Always report any damage, however small, to the landowner.
11 Do not leave litter.
12 Follow the country code.

COMMON SENSE MEASURES

1 Never go flying alone. If you have an accident there may be nobody to help you.
2 If you decide to fly off on a cross country flight, be sure to tell somebody beforehand approximately where you are going and when you hope to land.
3 If you go flying over water, wear a life jacket. The inflatable sort is the most useful for a hang glider pilot. Make sure that you can detach yourself easily from the glider after landing in the water and carry a knife in case you run into trouble. Unless the glider is fitted with floats it will be quite unmanageable in the water.
4 Before flying from a hill, have a good look for electricity power lines or telephone wires. Power lines will also be marked on the map. Beware of rocks, farm machinery, barbed wire and so forth in the landing area.
5 If you are flying in remote places, give a thought to survival in case you come down in an inaccessible place just before nightfall.

11 First Aid

If somebody has an accident while flying, you may be the only person available to help. Do not be afraid that because you have no experience of first aid, you may do the wrong thing or make things worse. First aid is mostly common sense.

In addition to administering first aid, however, you are uniquely placed to take note of what there is to see: what you observe may be of vital importance in deciding what went wrong. So try to remember what the pilot did, without inventing anything. Then look carefully at the position of the pilot and the glider, and try to memorise the details exactly; note any marks on the ground nearby and whether there is anything wrong or out of place on the glider. Only move what is necessary to free the pilot and remember its position before you touch it. As soon as possible afterwards, write it down. Report the accident to your Safety Officer and, if it is serious, to the police.

It is probable that an accident casualty will be on the ground, but it is possible that he will be in a tree, on a steep hillside or in water.

First, make sure that the casualty is safe and not likely to sustain further injury. It may be necessary to move him or release him from the glider. If he is conscious, he can tell you where he is hurt. If he is unconscious, move him carefully in case he has a back injury.

If he is not breathing

1 Loosen clothing at the neck.
2 Open the mouth and clear the airway by removing any mud, blood, loose teeth, vomit etc, and wipe mouth clean. Pull tongue forwards and lift chin.

This may be sufficient to start breathing, and is a life saving procedure. If not, start artificial respiration.

Artificial Respiration

1 Hold the chin forwards.
2 Pinch the nose with the other hand.
3 Tilt back the head and place your mouth over the mouth of the casualty so that your lips make a seal. Place a single thickness of handkerchief between mouths if you wish.
4 Breathe into the casualty's mouth as you breathe out. You will see his chest move.
5 Do this about once every five seconds. Lift your mouth off the casualty's mouth between each breath, to allow the air to change.
6 Continue until natural breathing is restored.

Unconscious Casualty Treat as if asleep.

1 Turn on to one side to prevent blood or vomit being inhaled – breathing is therefore unobstructed.
2 Straighten underneath leg.
3 Underneath arm by side.
4 Bend upper leg – this prevents the casualty rolling on to the back.
5 If injuries prevent this method, keep casualty on one side with something firm at the back.
6 Do not attempt to give drinks to an unconscious casualty.
7 It is not necessary to try to keep a casualty awake if he has been concussed by a blow on the head.

Bleeding

1 Lie casualty down with bleeding part higher than the chest.

2 Make a pad and place it on the bleeding area, bandage firmly. This will stop nearly all bleeding in about five minutes.
3 If the injury is very severe, such as a severed arm or leg, wrap some padding round the upper arm or thigh between the injury and the body. Tie a band over the padding. Put a stick under the band and twist to tighten just enough to stop blood spurting. Note the time. Release pressure after 20 minutes. If spurting reappears after one minute, tighten the band again for 20 minutes then release again.

Internal Injuries
1 If air is sucking into or out of a chest wound, cover the wound with a dressing.
2 If the casualty complains of severe pain in the neck or back, or is unable to move legs or arms or has numbness, there may be injuries to the spine. Move the casualty as little as possible. Improvise a stretcher. The position most comfortable is usually best.
3 Pain in the stomach may mean injuries to the internal organs or pelvis. Move with care.

Burns Possibly caused by the sun, by a cooking stove, by flying into electricity wires, or by touching frozen metal surfaces.
1 Spray or immerse the burned or frozen area in *cool water* for 15–20 minutes. *This will immediately reduce the pain and the extent of the injury.*
2 Put on a clean dry linen dressing.

If clothes are burning, push the casualty to the ground and smother flames with anything handy, or roll casualty on the ground and beat out the flames.

Broken Arms or Legs
1 Put the injured limb carefully into a comfortable position – you will *not* make it worse by doing this.
2 Cover open wounds with a clean dry dressing. Any clean cloth will do.
3 The legs can usually be tied together; one will act

as a splint for the other.

4 For arm injuries, make a sling.
5 A broken arm may sometimes be more comfortable if tied to the body.
6 Splints may be made from rolled up papers. Bind these gently, but securely, to the limb to hold the fracture steady.
7 For leg injuries, lie the casualty down with the legs slightly raised.
8 Dislocations: treat as fractures.

Shock (or Heart Attack) Some shock occurs in all accidents and is made worse by loss of blood.

1 Allow casualty to *lie undisturbed* so far as possible. (For a heart attack *sitting* on the ground is better.)
2 Covering with blankets is not necessary unless the casualty feels cold.
3 Cooling by fanning may be necessary in hot climates.

Shock will frequently pass off within a short time if the casualty is left undisturbed, provided that there is no bleeding.

No special treatment is required.

Drinks If the casualty is likely to be in hospital in less than a few hours give no food or drinks, not even water.

If there is likely to be a *long delay* before hospital treatment can be given, then drinks and even food may be essential.

It is better to give neither drinks nor food until you know what further treatment is necessary: it may require an anaesthetic. A casualty on a mountain or other isolated place may need drink or food. If you suspect internal injuries, use your judgement.

Equipment If you want to be prepared, keep a sling, a clean handkerchief, and a few elastic adhesive dressings in your pocket. A small pocket knife and a whistle might also be useful.

12 Useful Information

ASSOCIATIONS

British Hang Gliding Association
167A Cheddon Road
Taunton
Somerset TA2 7AH

US Hang Gliding Association
PO Box 66306
Los Angeles, CA 90066
USA

Australian Self Soar Association
PO Box 1706
Adelaide, Australia 5001

BOOK LIST

Hang Gliding by Dan Paynter (Paynter, Santa Barbara, California).
Meteorology for Glider Pilots by C E Wallington (John Murray).
Hang Gliding Catch the Wind by Glen Woodward (Angus and Robertson).
Hang Glider Pilot by Anne Welch and Gerry Breen (John Murray).
Hang Gliding by Martin Hunt and David Hunn (Pelham Books).

Glossary

AEROFOIL. A shape designed to produce lift when air flows over it.
AIRSPEED. Speed through the air, irrespective of speed over the ground.
ANGLE OF ATTACK. Angle at which wing meets the airstream in flight.
BANK. Angle between wings and horizontal. The verb 'to bank' means 'to roll'.
BATTENS. Stiffeners in the sailwing.
BOOMS. The main structural tubes of the glider.
CENTRE OF GRAVITY. The centre of gravity of the aircraft and pilot together.
CENTRE OF LIFT. The point in the aircraft through which the lift is deemed to operate. Properly called the centre of pressure.
CONTROL BAR. The triangular frame under the wing to which the rigging wires are attached, used to control the aircraft in flight.
CROSS WIND. Wind blowing across the flight path of the aircraft.
DRAG. Effect of air resistance holding aircraft back.
DRIFT. Movement of aircraft sideways over ground.
FIN. A fixed vertical surface on the fore and aft axis of the aircraft.
FLARE OUT. Gradual flattening of glide path prior to landing aircraft.
FLEXWING. An aircraft with a flexible sail to form the wing.
GLIDE ANGLE. The angle between the glide path of the aircraft and the horizontal.
GLIDING. Controlled flight using the force of gravity to provide the forward speed necessary to give lift.
GROUND SPEED. The speed of the aircraft over the ground irrespective of its speed through the air.
HEARTBOLT. The main bolt holding the glider components together, where keel, cross boom and control and king post are attached.
KING POST. The vertical tube projecting upwards from the keel boom to support the top rigging wires.
KITE. Commonly used description for a hang glider.
L/D RATIO. The ratio between lift and drag which gives the distance gained for height lost in still air.
LUFF. The collapse of the sail with loss of lift caused by the airstream striking the sail at a small or zero angle of attack.

MUSH. Loss of height just before aircraft stalls.

NOSE ANGLE. The angle between the leading edge booms.

NOSE PLATE. The plate to which the leasing edge booms are attached.

RIGID WING GLIDER. A glider with conventional rigid wings.

REFLEX. A curve in the upper surface of wing or boom to give it a saucer-like hollow.

RIDGE SOARING. Soaring in the lift produced by the wind blowing onto a hill side.

ROACH. Rounding the trailing edge of the wing tip to decrease tendency for the tip to stall.

ROGALLO. Usual name for the delta-shape hang glider with flexible wings originated by Dr Francis Rogallo.

ROLLING PLANE. The plane at right angles to the fore and aft axis around which the aircraft rolls.

ROTATE. Rotating the nose up or down.

ROTOR. The turbulent air found beyond the crest of a hill or below the lip of a cliff.

SINK RATE. Loss of height in feet or metres per second.

SLIP OR SIDESLIP. The aircraft slipping or skidding sideways so that the airstream does not strike the wings in a directly fore and aft line.

SOARING. Gliding in air which is rising faster than the glider is sinking.

SPIN. Uncontrolled descent with the aircraft spiralling in a stalled condition.

STABILITY. The tendency of the aircraft to resume a straight glide after being disturbed.

STALL. The breakdown of the airflow over the wings leading to loss of lift, and the aircraft falling.

THERMAL. A rising bubble of warm air which will continue to rise until it reaches the same temperature as the surrounding air.

TRACK. The path over the ground made good by the aircraft.

TRAILING EDGE. The rear edge of the wing.

WING AREA. Total projected area of the wing.

WING LOADING. The weight carried by each square foot of wing calculated as an average from the total weight and wing area. Quoted in pounds per square foot.